Table of Contents

Introduction

Successful Parenting is a book designed to enrich and greatly improve your parenting skills. It is also a *course in parenting* designed for parents who need help with their child's problem behavior.

The "Successful Parenting" approach incorporates developmental expectations of your child's behavior with the latest advances in the techniques of motivating and changing behavior. The course in this book is designed to teach you with "hands on" exercises to insure your success.

Throughout the book you will be prompted to takes notes and do exercises. Your doing the exercises in each chapter will be crucial to gaining a good understanding of the material covered and how the material applies to you and your child's situation. We encourage you to keep a notebook for doing the exercises as well as tracking your child's progress.

In this book you will learn about How Children Develop, What Effective Discipline Is, How to Change Inappropriate Behavior, and How to Strengthen Appropriate Behavior. In this course you will find introductions to these ideas, examples, and exercises which are designed to provide you with new tools for Successful Parenting.

This book is designed to better your parenting skills. Professionals in the fields of Child Development and Behavioral Psychology use many of the ideas and concepts in the book. While the material in this book will greatly improve your parenting skills, it is not intended to be a replacement for professional help. If you feel your child has a serious behavioral problem which may require professional help don't hesitate to contact a professional who specializes in children's behavioral problems.

What is Discipline?

The word discipline basically means to teach and learn. Through the centuries cultures have devised different ways to teach and learn. The way we teach and learn is important. Your key role as a parent is that of TEACHER. Knowing that our key role as parents is that of teacher we need to understand what teaching is and how best to do it. This will ensure our child's success at learning.

The *key element* in teaching is *motivation*. The method that is used to motivate a person plays the central role in how what is being taught is received or learned. Some people primarily motivate through methods of *reward* and others use methods that primarily motivate through *punishment*. All teaching styles use one or both of these methods.

When REWARD methods are used to teach the learning experience has greater impact. Reward methods are those typically associated with POSITIVE REINFORCEMENT. This will be discussed in greater detail in the chapter entitled "Positive Reinforcement".

When PUNISHMENT methods are used to teach something it produces one of two responses: ESCAPE or AVOIDANCE. Punishment should be used sparingly and only in the amount necessary. This will be discussed in greater detail in the chapter entitled "Escape / Avoidance".

Another *important element* to teaching is CONSISTANCY. If we take a close look at the meaning of this word consistency we discover that it means *agreement between acts or statements*; *making logical connections* and *not contradictory; compatible; harmonious, conforming to a single set of principles, or to previous action or belief.*

Children need to see the agreement between how you teach them in one situation with how you teach them in another similar situation. If there is *agreement* between both situations in how you teach them, then they make the logical connection that you will continue to teach them in the same manner in that kind of situation. The outcome of the situation becomes predictable for them. YOUR actions are not contradictory. There is harmony in your teaching. Your child can see that there is a set of principles in your teaching. They realize that they are conforming to your previous teaching.

Consistency is the backbone of effective parenting (teaching). Without it there is no success. The more consistent your are in using the principles and teaching techniques in this book the more success you will have. A key part of your job as the parent / guardian is being consistent. Your child's success will depend on it.

Another *important element* to teaching is realizing that *YOU, as the parent (or guardian), are the most important factor for producing change in your child*. This is because you have the power and authority to choose how your child will be taught in your home. Your child will follow your lead and respond to the environmental conditions you set into place. As you set goals for your child he will reach those goals as you provide him with the tools to do so.

The combination of understanding and using these *elements of teaching* and the ideas presented in this book will help you with effective discipline and *Success in Parenting*.

Your Child's Development

All living things develop as they grow and human beings are no exception. As children grow and develop they go through DEVELOPMENTAL STAGES. This simply means that children go through *Changes* in *periods of time* or *steps* as they grow. These Developmental Changes take place *Physically*, *Emotionally, Cognitively,* and *Socially.* These Changes give children *ABILITIES* to perform certain skills.

This book will focus more on you becoming familiar with your child's individual *abilities* within each of the Developmental areas instead of teaching you all of the many complex Stages of Development.

All children go through the same Changes (Stages). With each new Change new *abilities* appear. These abilities appear in each child within each child's individual developmental time line. In other words each child has his own individual speed at which he develops. For example: One child may begin walking at 10 months of age and another child may begin walking at 13 months of age. While both children attain the ability to walk they each walk when they are ready.

As you attempt to change your child's behavior or teach him new behaviors you must carefully consider his individual abilities. This means you simply consider your child's *abilities in the areas of his Physical, Emotional, Cognitive,* and *Social areas* of *Development.* As you become familiar with your child's Developmental Abilities you will be able to gain appropriate *Developmental Expectations* for making decisions about teaching him new behaviors and changing his undesirable behaviors. Let's look at each of these developmental areas a little closer:

PHYSICAL DEVELOPMENT: Physical refers to the physical body. Development refers to stages of growth. So when we talk about your child's Physical Development we are talking about his stages of physical growth. You can see your child's stages of physical growth by looking at his Physical Abilities.

As your child grows physically his coordination and other Physical Abilities improve. His Physical Abilities to perform tasks improves.

EMOTIONAL DEVELOPMENT: Emotional refers to your child's feelings. Development refers to stages of growth. So when we talk about your child's Emotional Development we are talking about the stages of feelings your child will go through as he grows. The way to identify your child's Emotional Development is to look at his *EMOTIONAL EXPRESSIONS.*

Understanding your child's Emotional Development plays a vital role in what you teach him and how you teach him. The responsibilities and privileges you give him should be directly related to his Stage of Development. His Emotional Expressions will give you clues as to his Stage of Development and over all emotional strength to cope with the new behaviors you want him to learn and the behaviors you want him to change. The younger your child is the weaker or more fragile his emotional strength is.

As your child grows emotionally his emotional strength to cope with learning new behaviors and changing undesirable behaviors will increase.

COGNITIVE DEVELOPMENT: Cognitive refers thinking or reasoning. Development refers to stages of growth. So when we talk about your child's Cognitive Development we are referring to his stages of thinking / reasoning ability.

Your child's ability to reason plays a vital role in his ability to accurately understand what you are trying to teach him.

SOCIAL DEVELOPMENT: Social refers to interaction between people. Development refers to stages of growth. So when we talk about your child's Social Development we are referring to his stages of interaction (between himself and others) that he will go through.

Your child's ability to interact with other children and adults determines the quality of relationship he will have with people.

As you begin to change your child's behavior or teach him new behaviors carefully consider his abilities within each of these areas. This careful consideration of his *Developmental Abilities* will guide you in *Developmental Expectations*. Your expectations of his behavior will be based on his actual abilities in each of these areas of development.

EXERCISES:

The following exercises are designed to help you recognize your child's *Developmental Abilities:*

PHYSICAL DEVELOPMENT:

Record on paper of the following:

Your child's age (both years and months old) and PHYSICAL DEVELOPMENT (ABILITIES). These are abilities which he has no problem performing. Use the following as a guideline: Physical Strength. Athletic Abilities. Coordination (Both Large Muscle & Eye-hand).

5

Here are some examples of what your list might look like:

A) *Michael, age 8 years and 7 months: Physical abilities:*
- *Ability to run fast.*
- *Ability to jump*
- *Ability to stand on one foot.*
- *Ability to ride a two-wheel bike.*
- *Ability to shoot a basketball into a low hoop and make a basket 2 out of 8 throws.*
- *Ability to color inside the lines when coloring in a coloring book.*
- *Ability to do fundamental skate boarding.*

B) *Steven, age 10 years and 2 months: Physical abilities:*
- *Ability to advance quickly on video game levels on first try (good eye-hand coordination).*
- *Ability to swim all the different kinds of swim strokes (including advanced strokes) required for his swim team.*
- *Ability to skate well with roller skates and skateboard.*
- *Ability to haul the large heavy trash cans out to the curb on trash day.*
- *Ability to carry the groceries from the car into the house by himself.*
- *Ability to reach almost all the cupboards in the kitchen.*
- *Ability to roller skate fairly well*

C) *Lisa, Age 4 years and 8 months: Physical abilities:*
- *Ability to ride her tricycle.*
- *Ability to climb to the top of her jungle gym at preschool.*
- *Ability to do two forward rolling tumbles.*
- *Ability to run fast.*
- *Ability to use scissors to cut out a circle.*
- *Ability to climb the ladder and go down the slide on her own.*
- *Ability to hang up her jacket using a hanger.*

These are just a few examples of how to make a list of your child's Physical Abilities. Don't try to make a comprehensive list. Keep it simple and short (about 7-12 items). This exercise is designed to help you become aware of your child's *Physical Development.* The more familiar you become with your child's Physical Development (Abilities) the better your *expectations* will become in your attempts to teach him new behaviors and change his undesirable behaviors.

EMOTIONAL DEVELOPMENT:

Record on paper of the following:

Your child's age (both in years and months) and EMOTIONAL EXPRESSIONS.

Use the following for a guideline:

- Does your child cry? How often? Under what circumstances does he usually cry?
- Does he laugh much? How often? What usually makes him laugh?
- How often does he get angry? Under what circumstances does he get angry?
- Does he express fear? How often and under what circumstances?
- How does he express his affection towards others? Is he verbal about his affections?
- What verbal expressions does he use to convey his affections towards others? In what circumstances does he show affections towards others? Does he physically show his affections? How? Towards whom and under what circumstances?
- Does your child express joy, happiness, and excitement? How often and under what circumstances?

There are many more categories that could be used here under Emotional Expressions. These are just a few to get you familiar with your child's *Emotional Development*. As you consider your child's *abilities* in his Emotional Development look at his *Emotional Expressions* (the ways in which he verbalizes and physically displays his happiness, excitement, anger, frustration, fear, affections, etc.). Here are some examples of how your list might look:

A) *Joey, age 6 years and 3 months: Emotional Expressions.*
- *Joey usually doesn't cry or wine that often. He cries when he is injured or when his older sister is teasing him great deal. He also cries sometimes if he is very tired.*
- *He usually laughs at cartoons and jokes. He frequently laughs when watching funny movies.*
- *Joey rarely gets angry. His outbursts of anger are usually confined only to being teased by his sister (or sometimes other kids).*
- *He usually expresses fear when his nightlight is accidentally turned off at bedtime.*
- *He is afraid of sleeping in a dark room. He is also afraid of pools and lakes because he can't swim.*
- *He is affectionate towards family members and his teacher at school.*
- *He likes to give and get hugs from us and on occasion, and sometimes his sister.*
- *He sometimes picks a flower for mom or his teacher at school. He designs and colors birthday cards for family members.*
- *He gets excited and a little hyper when the family is going to the park.*
- *He seems quite happy when he gets to go to his cousin's house across town.*
- *Joey has an expression he uses when he gets excited, It's "Wahoo!" When he says this we have a clue that he is excited about what is happening.*

7

B) *Sarah, age 5 years and 6 months: Emotional Expressions:*
- *Sarah seems to wine frequently.*
- *She usually to cries when mildly teased by her older brother or other children.*
- *She seems not to laugh that often.*
- *She is frightened easily. Especially by adults she doesn't know. She has to sleep with two night-lights on in her bedroom (because of the dark). She is afraid of dogs.*
- *When scared by something she usually tears up or starts to cry.*
- *When frightened she becomes very clingy with us. She wants us to hold her and not put her down.*
- *She is very affectionate with the family. She hugs us very frequently.*
- *She carries her stuffed rabbit around sometimes. She holds it close and sometimes hugs it.*
- *She usually gets excited when she gets to go play at her friend's house, next door (which is only about three times a week). She also gets excited sometimes when she goes to the mall (about twice a month).*

C) *Kathy, age 9 years and 4 months: Emotional Expressions:*
- *Kathy usually "tears up" if she sees something real sad (like an animal that dies or sad movie), and that's not very often.*
- *She usually only cries if she is injured or extremely embarrassed by others.*
- *She seems to laugh and giggle more with friends than with her family members.*
- *When she is with her friend Carla they seem to laugh and giggle a lot.*
- *She expresses fear of dark rooms, bugs, and especially spiders.*
- *She usually screams a little when she is surprised by a bug.*
- *She is very affectionate with the family and sometimes with her friends.*
- *She gives family members hugs frequently and tells us she loves us.*
- *She likes to hold her one-year-old baby brother and rock him frequently.*
- *She gets very excited when her friends stay the night. She and her friend will usually perform some kind of skit or song for the family. One way we know she gets excited is when she tends to talk louder.*

These are just a few examples of how to make a list of your child's Emotional Expressions. Keep your list simple and short (about 7-12 items). This exercise is designed to help you become aware of your child's Emotional Development. This will be important and have an impact as you make decisions about behaviors you want him to learn and the undesirable behaviors you want him to change.

COGNITIVE DEVELOPMENT:

Make a list on paper of the following:

Your child's age (both years and months) and his Cognitive Abilities. As mentioned earlier, Cognitive Ability refers to *REASONING ABILITY*. These are Reasoning Abilities which he has no problem performing. Use the following as a guideline:

- Reading skill level: Is he at or below his grade level? List reading habits at home.
- Math skill level: Is he at or below his grade level?
- Spelling skill level: Is he at or below his grade level?
- Can he tell time? How well? This applies typically to children 7 years of age or younger.
- Story telling or story writing skills. This means his ability to verbalize or write a fictional story or true events.

** *You will need your child's teacher's input to answer some of these.*

Here are some examples of how your list might look like:

A) *Kevin, Age 5 years and 3 months: Reasoning Abilities:*
- *Kevin can say all his ABC's.*
- *He recognizes most of the letters of the alphabet.*
- *He can count to 25.*
- *He can verbally spell his name.*
- *He recognizes his written name.*
- *He recognizes 12:00 noon and 3:00 p.m. on the clock.*
- *He knows four simple songs.*

B) *Alicia, Age 11 years and 4 months: Reasoning Abilities:*
- *Alicia's teacher reports Alicia is slightly below her grade level in reading.*
- *Alicia reads a short story book almost every night. The books range from fourth to fifth grade reading level.*
- *Alicia's teacher reports that Alicia is at her grade level in math.*
- *Alicia's teacher reports Alicia is slightly below her grade level in spelling*
- *Alicia can verbalize the events of her day in order and with great detail.*
- *She likes to create stories and tell them on video tap*
- *She can write short stories (about two pages long).*

C) *Carol, Age 12 years and 2 months: Reasoning Abilities:*
- *Her teacher reports she is at grade level in her reading.*
- *She reads one short book a week. These are books from her school library.*
- *She writes a one-page book report on each book.*

- *Her teacher reports she is at grade level in math.*
- *Her teacher reports she is at grade level in spelling.*
- *She can verbalize the events of her day in order and with good detail.*
- *She creates and writes a story about 4 pages long.*

These are just a few examples of how to make a list of your child's Cognitive Abilities. Keep your list simple and short (about 7-12 items). This exercise is designed to help you become aware of your child's Cognitive Development. This will be important and have an impact as you make decisions about behaviors you want him to learn or behaviors you want him to change.

SOCIAL DEVELOPMENT:

Make a list on paper of the following:

Your child's age (both years and months old) and his SOCIAL ABILITIES. These are abilities which he has no problem performing. Use the following for a guideline:

- The ability to share. What things does he share and under what circumstances?
- When confronted with a conflict with another child how often does he compromise, if needed, with the other child to solve the problem?
- Which circumstances of conflict is he most likely to compromise in?
- How often does he accept the decisions of the "Adult-in-Charge"? How often does he accept those decisions immediately and pleasantly?
- How often and under what circumstances does he display physical self-control when faced with a significant conflict with another child?
- How often and under what circumstances does he ask permission to play with or use another child's toy or personal property?
- How often does he ask the "Adult-In-Charge" or other child?
- How often and under what circumstances does he express his disapproval of what others are doing?

There are many more categories that could be used here under Social Development (Abilities). These are just a few to get you familiar with this specific area of your child's development. Here are a few examples of how your list might look:

A) *Eric, age 7 years and 2 months: Social Abilities:*
- *Eric shares his toys with his brother and sister usually when he is not interested in playing with the particular toy his brother or sister wants to use. He applies the same rule when playing with non-family members as well.*
- *When confronted with a very mild conflict with another child he can compromise, if needed, on occasion with that other child in order to resolve the conflict.*
- *Eric will accept the decisions of the adult-in-charge immediately and pleasantly*

about one out of every ten.

- *When confronted with a significant conflict with another child he displays physical self-control nine out of ten times provided that the other child has not been physical with him first.*
- *He will ask permission to play with another child's toy about once out of every times. When he does ask, he usually asks the adult-in-charge.*
- *When another child is doing something he disapproves of he will verbalize it most of the time.*
- *When the adult-in-charge does something that he disapproves of (such as setting limits or telling him "no") he will verbalize it about half of the time.*

B) *Katie, age 10 years and 4 months: Social Abilities:*
- *Katie shares her toys and other personal property with her sister about half of the time.*
- *She shares her toys and other personal property with her friends (when they are at our house) about eighty percent of the time.*
- *When confronted with a conflict with a child from another family she will compromise, if needed, about eight out of ten times.*
- *When confronted with a conflict with her older sister she will compromise, if needed, about twenty percent of the time.*
- *She will accept the decisions of the adult-in-charge about seventy percent of the time. Most of the time she accepts those decisions immediately and pleasantly.*
- *She displays physical self-control in all significant conflicts with other children.*
- *She will ask permission to play with or use another child's toy or personal property about three out of ten times. When asking permission she usually will ask the "adult-in-charge".*
- *When another child is doing something she disapproves of she will verbalize it immediately almost every time.*
- *When the adult-in-charge does something she disapproves of (such as setting limits or telling her "no") she will verbalize it about two out of ten times.*

C) *Melanie, age 12 years and 7 months: Social Abilities:*
- *Melanie shares her personal property with her younger sisters and brother when she can monitor its use closely.*
- *She will share a few items of her personal property with her friends occasionally.*
- *When confronted with a conflict with her siblings she will compromise, if needed about 6 out of 10 times. When confronted by a conflict with her friends she will compromise about nine out of ten times.*
- *She will accept the decisions of the adult-in-charge about nine out of ten*

times. She accepts most of those decisions immediately and pleasantly.

- *She displays physical self-control in all significant conflicts with other children.*
- *She will ask permission to use the property of other people about seven out of ten times.*
- *When another child is doing something she disapproves of she will verbalize it immediately most of the time. When the adult-in-charge does something she disapproves of she will verbalize it about four out of ten times.*

These are just a few examples of how to make a list of your child's Social Development (Abilities). Keep it short and simple (about 7-12 items). This exercise is designed to help you become aware of this area of your child's development. This will be important and have an impact as you make decisions about behaviors you want him to learn or behaviors you want him to change.

 For a more in depth look at the Stages of Development children check online for books dedicated to the Subject of Child Development. Such books can give you the many complex details of the Stages of Development.

CHAPTER SUMMARY: *Your understanding of your child's Physical, Emotional, Cognitive, and Social Development is crucial for making healthy decisions about your child's learning new behaviors and changing undesirable behaviors. The more familiar you become with your child's areas of development and his abilities in each of these areas the better your expectations of his behavior will become in your attempts to teach him new behaviors and change his undesirable behaviors. Your deeper understanding of your child's development and better expectations of him will give you Success in Parenting.*

What is Behavior?

When we talk about your child's behavior we are referring to anything you can <u>observe</u> your child do which you can <u>record</u> and <u>measure</u>. This means physical actions such as running, sitting, holding, crying, laughing, etc. (action words).

The emotions your child experiences are internal feelings. You cannot observe your child's emotions. You can only observe how they make your child act (physically). The focus of this book is on changing your child's *actions* or teaching him new actions.

OBSERVING / RECORDING / MEASURING

Now that we know that behavior is something we can observe, record, and measure, let's discuss each of these.

OBSERVATION: When you observe your child you see him with your eyes and hear him with your ears.

EXAMPLES:

> A) You see your eight-year-old son <u>drop</u> his red jacket on the back porch, <u>open the back door</u> and <u>run through the kitchen.</u>

> B) You see your six-year-old daughter <u>pick up</u> the blue towel, <u>wrap it around he shoulders</u>, and <u>run down the hallway yelling: "I'm super woman!"</u>

Notice in these examples how what was seen and heard are the only things recorded. Notice how the emotions of the children are not mentioned. This is because the focus here is the outward behavior (actions) of the child. These are descriptions of the children's <u>physical actions</u>.

OBSERVATIONS GUIDELINES:

1) Use your eyes to observe.

2) Use your ears to observe.

3) Focus in on your child's physical actions, not his emotions (feelings).

RECORDING: Recording your child's behavior simply involves writing down on paper what your child's behavior is. This book will teach you the basic skills for recording your child's behavior. First, let's look at some short examples of some recordings of some parents.

EXAMPLES:

A) One father writes: *I asked John to please put the plate on the counter in the kitchen. John replied, I don't have too, that's Sally's job!" John then ran out of the living room.*

B) One mother writes: *Shelly asked Mike where her doll was. Mike said he did not know. Shelly then kicked Mike in the leg. Mike struck Shelly on her arm with his fist. Shelly screamed: Mom, Mike hit me!"*

C) One mother writes: *Adam sat his books on the coffee table, then picked up the T.V. remote and put it in his left pant pocket. He then left the living room and went to his bed room, where he stayed for an hour.*

Notice that each recording states <u>what each child did</u>. There are no statements that <u>put a label on the children</u>. The recordings are not stating that the child was " bad ", "good", or "being a brat", etc. The recordings simply state the physical actions of the children.

You can also use a video camera to record your child's behavior. The best way to do this is to set the camera in a place where it will not distract your child. Then let the camera record your child's behavior for a designated period of time. Later you can review the videotape and record your observation on paper.

RECORDING GUIDELINES:

1. When you record your child's behavior avoid using CHARACTER / ATTITUDE LABELS. Character / Attitude Labels are terms that people use to describe the child's character or attitude. These labels are terms like: bad, good, careless, rude, being a brat, stubborn, lazy, selfish, rebellious, etc. Putting labels on children does not give you Objective Information. Objective Information is what you will need to have when you <u>TARGET</u> behavior. We will discuss this more in the chapter on "Targeting Behavior".

2. Stick to describing your child's <u>physical and verbal actions</u> (use verbs).

3. Put down the date, time and location of the observation. Make sure you put the starting and ending time of the observation. This information will also be useful.

14

4. Only record information that will be useful. Remember, you are not writing a book.

The recording is a <u>short overview</u> of your child's physical and verbal behavior within a short designated period of time.

MEASURING: Measuring your child's behavior is the process of *categorizing* and *counting* particular behaviors. Counting the behaviors can also involve counting the time periods in which a particular behavior occurs.

EXAMPLES:

    A) Bobby dropped his spoon 4 times at dinner.

    B) Carol through the ball 6 times.

    C) Kelly left his bike outside overnight 4 times in the last 7 days.

    D) Adam brushed his teeth for 2 minutes.

    E) Debbie hung her sweater up after school 4 times this week (5-day week).

    F) Drew watched T.V. quietly for 15 minutes.

MEASURING GUIDELINES:

1. Underline the action words in your recording. Then make a list of these action word putting them into categories (such as: running, jumping, talking, etc).

2. Count the number of times your child engaged in each category of behavior. After counting the times each behavior occurred in each category record your results.

EXERCISE FOR OBSERVING / RECORDING / MEASURING:

Do the following exercise 5 times:

1. Observe your child for twenty minutes. While you are observing record (write down on paper) your child's actions. <u>Follow the guidelines for Observing and Recording.</u>

2. After you are done recording your child's behavior on paper underline the *action word* or *action phrases* in your recording.

3. Make a category for each behavior *(action word* or *action phrase).*

4. Now count each time your child engaged in each of these Categories of Behavior and write down the results.

After completing this exercise you will have the basic skills it takes to gather the necessary information you will need to help you make decisions about changing your child's behavior. The following are examples of this exercise:

EXAMPLE A:
Saturday, September 29, 1996
Time: 9:15am
Location: Living room, Kitchen, Front Yard

9:15am: Craig, age 8, is sitting on the floor a few feet from the T.V. Watching cartoons. He is sitting quietly.

9:22am: Craig gets up from watching T.V. and walks into the kitchen. He then <u>opens the refrigerator</u> and gets out a soda. He takes four drinks of the soda, puts it back into the refrigerator and shuts the door. He then <u>runs</u> back into the living room <u>yelling</u> "whoopee", <u>jumps onto the couch</u> and begins to watch T.V. again.

9:26am: Craig <u>stands up on the couch</u>, <u>jumps off</u> and <u>runs</u> to the front door. He opens the front door and runs outside <u>leaving the door open</u>.

9:30am: Craig <u>runs back into the house slamming the front door</u> as he enters. He then <u>runs</u> into the kitchen, <u>opens the refrigerator door</u>, grabs his soda, takes one long drink, puts the soda back, shuts the refrigerator door, and <u>runs</u> back into the living room where he <u>jumps onto the couch</u>. He picks up the remote and changes the channel. Craig is now sitting quietly.

9:35: Observation is over.

Now let's categorize Craig's behavior:

1. Study the observation. We have picked out the behaviors (these are action words or phrases which we do not want Craig doing).

2. After picking out these action words and phrases we underlined each of them.

3. After underlining these words and phrases we make a list of them.

4. This list now becomes our Categories of Behaviors we want changed. This list (Categories of Behaviors) contains our TARGET BEHAVIORS. Target Behaviors are behaviors you want your child to either change or learn. In this case we have chosen behaviors we want Craig to change.

***Our Categories of Behaviors for Craig should look like the following:

CATEGORIES OF BEHAVIORS FOR CRAIG

These are inappropriate behaviors we want Craig to change:

1	Opens refrigerator door (without adult permission.	2 Times
2	Running in the house.	5 Times
3	Yelling in the house.	1 Time
4	Jumping on the furniture.	3 Times
5	Standing on the furniture.	1 Time
6	Leaving the front door open.	1 Time
7	Slamming doors.	1 Time

Here we can see that Craig engaged in 7 different inappropriate behaviors. These behaviors occur a total of 14 times. This is important information. It can tell us which behaviors we need to work on. Notice how the observation *did not* contain *labels* of his character or attitude.

Some may ask why we are only focusing in on Craig's *inappropriate* behavior instead of his appropriate behavior. The reason for this is we are looking at what behaviors we want to **change**. While it is true that you can focus in on your child's appropriate behaviors in your recordings, the main reason for recording behavior is to focus in on the inappropriate behaviors you want changed.

EXAMPLE B:
Monday, September 31, 1996
Time: 4:30pm
Location: Living room:

4:30pm: Ashley, age 10, is sitting quietly on the sofa watching T.V. She is asked to go clean up the mess she made in the kitchen. <u>Ashley does not respond to the request</u>. Her eyes are fixed on the T.V. She is asked for a second time to go and clean up the mess she made in the kitchen. <u>Ashley does not respond to the request</u>. She sits with her eyes fixed on the T.V.

4:40pm: Ashley is still sitting on the couch watching T.V. For a third time she is asked to go clean up the mess she made in the Kitchen. <u>She does not respond to the request</u>. She is sitting quietly with her eyes fixed on the T.V.

4:45: Ashley gets up from the couch, goes into the kitchen, and takes some cookies from the cookie jar. She then goes into her bedroom.

4:47pm Ashley is in her room. She is told for a fourth time to go clean up the mess she made in the kitchen. Ashley responds saying: "<u>I do not have to clean up my mess in the kitchen because I did dishes last night</u>." Ashley then leaves her room quickly <u>slamming the door</u> behind her. <u>The request for cleaning up her mess was ignored</u>.

4:50pm: Ashley is in the kitchen sitting at the table eating more cookies. She is asked to clean up the mess she made before she leaves the kitchen. <u>She does not</u> <u>respond to the request.</u> She sits staring out the window watching her friends play outside.

4:53pm: Observation is over.

Now let's categorize Ashley's behavior:

1. Study the observation. We have picked out the behaviors (These are action words or phrases) which we do not want Ashley doing.

2. We have underlined the action words and phrases.

3. After underlining these action words and phrases we made a list of them.

4. This list now becomes our Categories of Behaviors we want changed. This list (Categories of Behaviors) contains our TARGET BEHAVIORS. Target Behaviors are behaviors you want your child to either <u>change</u> or <u>learn</u>. In this

case we have chosen behaviors we want Ashley to change.

***Our Categories of Behaviors for Ashley should look like the following:

CATEGORIES OF BEHAVIORS FOR ASHLEY

These are the inappropriate behaviors we want Ashley to change:

BEHAVIOR:	HOW MANY TIMES:
1) Ignoring the Adult-In-Charge.	5 times
2) Back talk.	1 time
3) Slamming the door.	1 time

Here we can see that Ashley engaged in 3 different inappropriate behaviors. These behaviors took place a total of 7 times. This is important information. It can tell us which behaviors we need to work on. Notice how the observation *did not* contain *labels* of her character or attitude. Remember that we are recording her behavior to focus in on the inappropriate behavior. The reason for this is we are looking at the behaviors we want **changed**.

EXAMPLE C:
Saturday, March 22, 1997
Time: 7:30pm
Location: Bathroom, bedroom.

Chris, age 11, is told to go take his evening shower. Chris responds: "I don't have to take one tonight, I took one last night." Chris is reminded he needs to take his shower every night. He goes to the bathroom and slams the door behind him. He turns on the bathroom radio very loud and takes his shower. After his shower he exits the bathroom dripping wet with his towel around him. As he heads for his bedroom he leaves a trail of water on the carpet. One look at the bathroom reveals that the shower curtain was left outside the tub when he showered and the floor is flooded. His clothes are on the floor and the radio is still playing very loud.

7:45pm: Chris has his pajamas on and is sitting in the living room watching T.V. He is asked to go clean the bathroom up and turn off the radio. <u>He does not respond to the request.</u> He sits silently starring at the T.V.

8:00pm: Chris is asked a second time to clean up the bathroom and turn off the radio. <u>Again, he does not respond to the request.</u>

8:10pm: Chris goes to the bathroom and turns off the radio. He then goes to his bedroom where he begins to play video games.

8:12pm: Observation is over.

Now let's look at Chris's behavior:

1. Study the observation. We have picked out the behaviors (These are action words or phrases) which we do not want Chris doing.

3. We have underlined the action words and phrases.

4. After underlining these words and phrases we make of list of them.

5. This list now becomes our Categories of Behaviors we want changed. This list (Categories of Behaviors) contains our TARGET BEHAVIORS. Target Behaviors are behaviors that you want your child to either <u>change</u> or <u>learn</u>. In this case we have chose behaviors we want Chris to change.

**Our Categories of Behaviors for Chris should look like the following:

<u>CATEGORIES OF BEHAVIORS FOR CHRIS</u>

These are inappropriate behaviors we want Chris to change.

BEHAVIOR:	**HOW MANY TIMES:**
1. Back-talk.	1 Time
2. Slamming door.	1 Time
3. Playing the radio loudly.	1 Time
4. Dripping water on the carpet.	1 Time
5. Leaving shower curtain outside tube when showering.	1 Time
6. Ignoring adult-in-charge.	2 Times

Here we can see that Chris engaged in 6 different inappropriate behaviors. These behaviors occurred a total of 7 times. This is important information. <u>It can tell us which behaviors we need to work on</u>. Notice how the observation *did not* contain labels of his <u>character</u> or <u>attitude</u>. Remember that our recording is focusing in on the inappropriate behavior instead of the appropriate behavior. The reason for this is we are focusing in on the behaviors we want **changed.**

CHAPTER SUMMARY: *It is vital to remember that your child's Behavior is something that you can observe, record, and measure. Recording your child's behavior on paper is often crucial in order to make the most objective decision. Following the Guidelines for observing, recording, and measuring will help to insure your success. Once you have studied this chapter and completed all the exercises you will be a step closer to Success in Parenting.*

The ABC'S of Behavior

The "A" stands for ANTECEDENT, the "B" stands for BEHAVIOR, and the "C" stands for Consequence.

ANTECEDENT: This is any condition or event that is present or occurring before a particular behavior. It is the setting and people involved.

BEHAVIOR: Any action that can be observed, recorded, and measured.

CONSEQUENCE: This is a condition or event that occurs after a particular behavior. It is the Consequence that follows the behavior that determines if the behavior will occur again and, if it does, how often. Always remember that *Behavior is maintained, weakened, or strengthened by Consequences.*

EXAMPLES:

A) Jimmy is playing with his trucks on the carpet while his older brother is watching T.V. in the same room a few feet from him. Jimmy picks up one of his trucks and throws it at his brother, who is sitting quietly on the couch. Jimmy's brother begins to cry. Jimmy's mother walks in the room and sees that Jimmy's brother is crying. The older brother tells the mother what Jimmy did. Mother then tells Jimmy to go to his room for 1 hour for throwing a truck at his brother.

Let's take a look at the Antecedent, Behavior, and Consequence in example "A". The behavior we are considering here is *Jimmy throwing the truck at his brother.*

The Antecedent: Jimmy is playing with his trucks on the floor a few feet from his older brother who is watching T.V. quietly.

The Behavior: Jimmy throws the truck at his brother.

The Consequence: Jimmy's brother begins to cry and Jimmy is sent to his room by his mother.

B) A father is shopping with his four-year-old girl in the super market. The girl sees a candy bar she wants. She asks her father for the candy.   The father tells the girl no. The child begins to cry. The father ignores her. After the girl cries for 5 minutes the father gives her the candy. The girl stops crying.

Let's take a look at the Antecedent, Behavior, and Consequence in example

"B". The behavior we are considering here is *the child crying for the candy*.

The Antecedent: The father and girl are shopping when the girl asks her father for a candy bar.

The Behavior: The behavior is the girl crying for the candy.

The Consequence: The consequence is the father gives the girl the candy and the crying stops.

C) Six-year-old Stacy sits quietly for an hour in the beauty salon while her mother gets her hair styled. When her mother is done she tells Stacy what a wonderful job she did sitting quietly for so long. Her mother then takes her for ice cream for doing so well at sitting quiet for so long.

Let's look at the Antecedent, Behavior, and Consequences in example "C". The behavior we are considering here is *Stacy sitting quietly for an hour*.

The Antecedent: The Antecedent is Stacy and her mother in the beauty salon.

The Behavior: The Behavior is Stacy sitting quietly for an hour.

The Consequence: The Consequence is Stacy's mother giving her verbal praise and taking her for ice cream.

D) Eight-year-old Kelly is asked by his father to clean his room. Within 30 minutes Kelly cleans his room. When his father comes in to inspect Kelly's job he smiles real big   and exclaims with great excitement: "Look at this room! You cleaned it so fast! Kelly you did a great job son! All of your clothes are put away! All of your toys are put in the right place! Your bed looks like a professional made it! Son, I am so proud of your work!" Kelly looks up at his dad and smiles as he absorbs his father's praise.

Let's look at the Antecedent, Behavior, and Consequence, in example "D". The behavior we are considering is *Kelly cleaning his room well within 30 minutes.*

The Antecedent: The Antecedent is Kelly being asked to clean his bedroom.

The Behavior: The Behavior is Kelly cleaning his room well in 30 minutes.

The Consequence: The Consequence is Kelly's father giving him verbal praise for a job well done.

As we said earlier, it is the consequence that affects behavior the most. The **consequence** will either maintain a particular behavior, weaken it, or strengthen it. Always consider these important keys when you are looking at the consequences of a particular behavior:

A) If an inappropriate behavior is followed by an appropriate punishment it will decrease (Weaken) the inappropriate behavior.

B) If an inappropriate behavior is followed by Positive Reinforcement (*pleasant* event) it will maintain or strengthen the inappropriate behavior.

C) If an appropriate behavior is followed by punishment it will decrease (weaken) the appropriate behavior.

D) If an appropriate behavior is followed by Positive Reinforcement (*pleasant* event) then the appropriate behavior will be maintained or strengthened.

DO THE FOLLOWING EXERCISE TWO TIMES:

Observe another parent and child in a situation in which a child is behaving appropriately. Observe the child's appropriate behavior and watch carefully for the consequence of that behavior. Write your observation down. Then underline the following:

A) What happened before that behavior (The setting and who is involved).

B) The appropriate behavior displayed.

C) The consequence that followed the appropriate behavior.

DO THE FOLLOWING EXERCISE TWO TIMES:

Observe another parent and child in a situation in which the child is behaving inappropriately. Observe the child's inappropriate behavior and watch carefully for the consequence of that behavior. Write your observation down. Then underline the following:

A) What happened before the behavior (the setting and who is involved).

B) The inappropriate behavior displayed.

C) The consequences that followed the inappropriate behavior. Be accurate with your answer.

DO THE FOLLOWING EXERCISE:

After completing the first two exercises of observing and recording other parents and their children do a similar exercise on you and your child. Do two observations and recordings in which your child behaved inappropriately and another two in which your child behaved appropriately. In the first two exercises you may have been able to record what you saw as you observed the other parents and their children. This part of the exercise will require that you do your recording after the events happen. Try to record your observation as soon as the events are over. After you record each observation underline the following:

A) What happened before the behavior (the setting and who is involved).

B) The behavior displayed.

C) The consequences that followed the behavior.

CHAPTER SUMMARY: *Learning the ABC's of Behavior is vital to your becoming an effective parent. To truly understand what causes behavior to be strengthened, maintained or weakened you first have to accurately identify the Antecedent, Behavior, and Consequence. The more you record your child's behavior and identify the "ABC's" the more effective you will become at managing the consequences of your child's behavior. It is imperative to remember that the consequences that follow a behavior will strengthen, maintain, or weaken that behavior. Managing the consequences of your child's behavior effectively will give you Success in Parenting.*

Positive Reinforcement

When a behavior is followed by a positive consequence then the behavior is strengthened. This means that the behavior is more likely to occur again in the future. Psychologists call this POSITIVE REINFORCEMENT.

The word POSITIVE refers to something *PLEASANT.* An important rule to remember is, *what is pleasant to one person may not be pleasant to another person.* Each person decides what is pleasant to him or her.

When you think of the word REINFORCEMENT, think of a beam which supports the main part of a building. The whole idea of Reinforcement is that something is strengthened, strongly supported, held up, etc.

Combing these together we can see POSITIVE REINFORCEMENT in action.

EXAMPLES:

A) Four-year-old Timmy is in the supermarket with his dad. He asks his dad for a candy bar and his dad tells him no. He then proceeds to cry. After five minutes of crying his dad gives him the candy bar. Upon receiving the candy Timmy stops crying.

This is a good example of the behavior of "crying" being **Positively Reinforced.** If we use the ABC's (Antecedent, Behavior, and Consequence) of Behavior to look at this situation we see the following:

Antecedent: Dad and Timmy are shopping. Timmy asks his dad for a candy bar and his dad says no.

Behavior: Timmy cries for five minutes.

Consequence: Dad gives Timmy the candy bar (the candy is the ***pleasant thing***).

A pleasant thing (candy) has followed the behavior of "crying". The "crying" behavior has been Positively Reinforced. Now the chances of Timmy "crying" in these circumstances in the future are greatly increased.

B) Seven-year-old Jennifer is sitting at her desk quietly and working hard at her spelling assignment for twenty minutes. This is very unusual for Jennifer as she is usually very talkative with other classmates and has a very difficult time staying in her chair for any length of time. After her teacher observes her sitting quietly and working hard for twenty minutes he walks over to her and comments: "You're doing super, you are working so quietly! I can tell you're working hard on your spelling, I really like that". Jennifer gives a big smile as she absorbs her teacher's praise.

This is a good example of "sitting quietly and working hard" behaviors being Positively Reinforced. If we use the ABC's (Antecedent, Behavior, and Consequence) of Behavior to look at the situation we see the following:

Antecedent: Jennifer's teacher gives her a spelling assignment.

Behavior: Jennifer sits quietly working hard for twenty minutes.

Consequence: Teacher gives Jennifer verbal praise.

The behaviors of sitting quietly and working hard have been followed by a **pleasant event (verbal Praise).** These behaviors have been Positively Reinforced. The chances of these behaviors occurring again in the future are greatly increased.

C) Its Saturday morning and ten-year-old Jimmy wants to go to the public pool which opens at 11:00am. His dad tells him he must have his room cleaned by 10:00am if he wants to go to the pool when it opens. Jimmy works hard to clean his room well and finishes by 9:45am. At 10:00am Jimmy's dad sees that the room has been cleaned well and on time. Jimmy's dad takes him to the pool when it opens.

This is a good example of "cleaning a room well and on time" being Positively Reinforced. If we use the ABC's (Antecedent, Behavior, and Consequence) of Behavior to look at this situation we see the following:

Antecedent: Ten-year-old Jimmy is told by his father that if he gets his room clean by 10:00am he can go to the public pool when it opens.

Behavior: Jimmy cleans his room well and on time.

Consequence: Jimmy's dad takes him to the pool when it opens at 11:00am.

The behaviors of "cleaning the room well and doing it on time" have been followed by a **pleasant** event (going to the pool). These behaviors have been Positively Reinforced. The chances of these behaviors occurring in the future are greatly increased.

D) Twelve-year-old Kevin's mother asked him to do his chore (the dinner dishes). He finishes his chore early and does a good job. Upon his mother's inspection of his chore his mother smiles at him and tells him: "Kevin, you've done a great job. This kitchen is cleaner than before I started cooking dinner. You not only get your chores done fast, but I love your attention to detail. Thank you for doing your chores so well". Kevin smiles back at his mother as he absorbs her praise.

This is a great example of the behaviors of "doing the dinner dishes quickly and with close attention to detail" being Positively Reinforced. If we use the ABC's (Antecedent, Behavior, and Consequence) of Behavior to look at the situation we see the following:

Antecedent: Kevin is asked by his mother to do his chore (the dinner dishes).

Behavior: He does them quickly and with attention to detail.

Consequence: Kevin's mother gives him verbal praise for a job done quickly and with attention to detail.

The behaviors of "doing the dinner dishes quickly and with attention to detail" have been followed by a **pleasant** event (mother's verbal praise). These behaviors have been Positively Reinforced. The chances of these behaviors occurring in the future have been greatly increased.

Now that we have seen how Positive Reinforcement works, let's look as some quick and effective ways to use it to teach your child new behavior and change your child's inappropriate behavior.

USING PRAISE FOR POSITIVE REINFORCEMENT

One of the quickest and most powerful ways of using Positive Reinforcement is to use *Praise*. Using Praise is simply letting your child know that you acknowledge his appropriate behavior and letting him know it's the kind of behavior that you value. Using Praise consist of making pleasant *Affirmative Statements* to your child or using *Affirming Physical Gestures* with your child. When Praise follows appropriate behavior then there is a strengthening of the appropriate behavior. The more you use Praise following your child's appropriate behavior the more his appropriate behavior will increase. The following is a list of examples of *Affirmative Praise Statements* and *Affirming Physical Gestures:*

AFFIRMATIVE PRAISE STATEMENTS:

- Thank you very much!
- You are doing a marvelous job!
- That's cleaning up your room really well.
- That's very clever of you!
- That's an impressive job.
- I really like the way you are doing that.
- Now you've got the hang of it.
- I like the way you are working!
- You're doing much better!
- You are doing superior work!
- You've got it now!
- Keep up the good work.
- You are on the right track now.
- That's right! Good for you!
- This is the kind of work that pleases me very much!
- I can see you have worked very hard on this!
- Very interesting!
- I like the way you said please.
- That's quite an improvement!
- Good job!
- I like the way you're being so patient with your brother.
- Look how fast you got this done, this is great!
- Good thinking!
- That's coming along very nicely.
- I like the way you are working so hard!
- I like the way you said thank you!
- I like the way you are waiting very quietly.
- You are such a hard worker!
- It's a pleasure to teach when you work like this!
- You have cleaned that so well!
- You make me smile when I see your good work!

AFFIRMING PHYSICAL GESTURES:

- A pat on the shoulder.
- A wink of the eye.
- A smile
- A hug
- A kiss on the cheek.
- A high-five handclasp.
- A pat on the head.
- A pat on the back.

EXERCISE:

The following exercise is designed to help you use Praise effectively:

1. Make a list of the Praise Statements and Affirming Physical Gestures you use with your child. The definition of Affirmative means to declare that which is positive and true and that which establishes the opposite of a negative. If you find you can't come up with many use those from the two lists above.

2. Keep a log for one full day of all the Praise Statements and Affirming Physical Gestures you used with your child immediately following his

appropriate behavior. Make a note of how many times this occurred.

3.   After you have made a log of one day spend the next 5 days increasing your Praise Statements and Affirming Physical Gestures. Each day try to double the number of Praise Statements and   Affirming Physical Gestures from the day before. Each day make a record of your progress. By the end of the 5-day period you will have a greater understanding of how Praise and Physical Affirmation can affect appropriate behavior. You should see significant changes in your child's behavior over the 5-day period. If you do not see significant changes keep increasing the amount of times you use Praise Statements and Physical Affirmation. You may think that your child does not engage in a lot of appropriate behavior that presents the opportunity for Positive Reinforcement. However, if you take the time to observe your child closely you will see plenty of opportunities to use these types of Positive Reinforcement. You can easily use Praise 3 or more times for just one appropriate behavior (such as sitting quietly and watching T.V. or doing a chore). <u>Praise and Physical Affirmation has its greatest results when it is used very frequently (many times an hour)</u>. The more you use Praise and Physical Affirmation to Positively Reinforce your child's appropriate behavior the more dramatic change you will see in your child. Make sure that your Praise comes after the appropriate behavior.

** **Make sure you avoid the pit fall of negative statements. This includes Sarcastic statements. Here are some examples:**

   - I sure am glad you're not that stupid!
   - I am glad you're not an idiot like your sister!
   - It's about time you got that right!
   - Finally, you're doing it right!
   - It's about time you did your work right!
   - It's about time you got your room clean on time!
   - I am amazed you actually got your work done!
   - If you cleaned your room like your sister, you could do it right.
   - I wish you could do better.
   - I told you so!

** Also avoid the pit fall of reinforcing inappropriate behavior. Since we have learned that behavior are maintained and strengthened by consequences <u>never use Praise immediately</u> <u>following your child's inappropriate behavior</u>. If you do you will reinforce his undesirable behavior.

USING THE REINFORCER LIST AND INCENTIVE CHARTS
FOR POSITIVE REINFORCEMENT

Another quick and powerful way to use Positive Reinforcement is to use a **Reinforcer List**. The Reinforcer List is a *list of opportunities* that your child enjoys. The list is called a "Reinforcer List" because these opportunities are used as **Positive Reinforcers**. **Positive Reinforcers are what make Positive Reinforcement work.** Remember how Positive Reinforcement works: *When a behavior is followed by a positive (Pleasant) consequence (Activity or thing) the behavior is strengthened.* After the list is made then each item on the list is identified as a *Daily*, *Weekly*, and *Monthly* (or long term) Reinforcer. Each Reinforcer is identified by putting a "D" (for Daily), "W" (for Weekly), and "M" (for Monthly) next to it. The reason for this is to designate which Reinforcers your child can earn on a Daily, Weekly, and Monthly basis.

Your child then earns each item on the list as a Positive Reinforcer as he displays appropriate behavior. He earns the Daily Reinforcers for meeting behavioral criteria for each day. He earns Weekly Reinforcers for meeting behavioral criteria for the week's period. He earns Monthly (or long term) Reinforcers for meeting behavioral criteria for the month (or long term).

Once the Reinforcer Lists are made then the Reinforcers are displayed on **INCENTIVE CHARTS**. The Reinforcer Lists and Incentive Charts work together as a powerful tool for teaching your child new behaviors and changing your child's inappropriate behavior. Incentive Charts will be discussed in detail in the next section.

The following is an exercise designed to teach you how to make Reinforcer Lists:

EXERCISE:

Make a list of all the activities and things your child enjoys doing. It can be ANY activity or thing your child enjoys (from special privileges to their favorite toys). You can also include a particular toy or other item he has been wanting you to buy for him. It is best to use activities and privileges that are already common in his life. The goal is to make your child's common "well-liked" daily, weekly and monthly activities and things contingent upon appropriate behavior. Here just a few examples of Reinforcers:

- T.V. / Videos.
- Riding bike.
- Riding skate boards.
- Riding horses.
- Going to the park.
- Special visits to friend's house.
- Going shopping.
- Baking cookies.
- Playing with the Lego set.

- Doing special arts & crafts.
- Staying up at night for an extra hour.
- Going miniature golfing.
- Video games.
- Roller blades, skates.
- Going to the beach.
- Using the stereo.
- Spend the night at a friend's house.

31

- Have a friend stay overnight.
- Going swimming.
- Purchase of a particular toy.
- Special food treats.

- Earning money to spend.
- Going to the movies.
- Going fishing.

This is just a short list. The sky is the limit because there are as many different kinds of Positive Reinforcers as there are children. Each child will have many activities and things they like. As you make your child's list take time to carefully consider all the activities he likes.

2. After making your child's list then put a **"D"** (for Daily), **"W"** (for Weekly) and **"M"** (for Monthly) next to each item on the list.

3. Next, divide the list into three separate lists. The first list will contain the Daily Reinforcers. The second list will contain the Weekly Reinforcers. The third list will contain the Monthly (or long term) Reinforcers.

Let's look at some examples:

A) The mother of nine-year-old Lisa made the following Reinforcer List:

Lisa's Reinforcer List

1. Riding bike. - (D)
2. Swimming.   - (W)
3. Computer games. - (D)
4. Going to cousin's house on Saturday. - (W)
5. Using Mom's needlepoint kit. - (D)
6. Renting Special Videos. - (W)
7. Baking cookies. - (W)
8. Collecting Barbie clothes. - (M)
9. Watching T.V. - (D)
10. Getting new fish for her fish tank. - (M)
11. Play with neighbors. - (D)
12. Use mom's watercolor paints. - (D)
13. Spend $5.00 at the dollar store. - (M)
14. Spend the night at friend's house. - (W)

Lisa's Daily Reinforcer List

1. Ride Bike.
2. Computer Games.
3. Use mom's needlepoint kit.
4. Watching T.V. over 1 hour.
5. Play with neighbors.
6. Use mom's watercolor paints.

Lisa's Weekly Reinforcer List

1. Going swimming.
2. Rent a special video.
3. Bake cookies.
4. Spend the night at friend's house.
5. Going to cousin's house on Saturday.

Lisa's Monthly Reinforcer List

1. Collect new Barbie clothes (Buy one new outfit).
2. Get new fish for fish tank.
3. Spend $5.00 at the Dollar store.

B) The father of eight-year-old Hector has made the following Reinforcer List:

Hector's Reinforcer List

1. Nintendo. - (D)
2. Riding bike. - (D)
3. Playing with friends. - (D)
4. Watching T.V. - (D)
5. Renting special videos. - (W)
6. Staying the night at a friend's house or having a friend sleep over. - (W)

7. Collecting Hot Wheels cars. - (M)
8. Going to Mc Donald's. - (W)
9. Collecting Action Figures. - (M)
10. Drinking sodas. - (D)
11. Using dad's dartboard (with supervision). - (W)
12. Staying up an extra hour at night. - (W)
13. Using the internet. - (D)

Hector's Daily Reinforcer List

1. Playing Nintendo.
2. Ride bike.
3. Play with friends.
4. Watch T.V. over 1 hour.
5. Drink sodas.
6. Use the Internet.

Hector's Weekly Reinforcer List

1. Rent a special video.
2. Stay the night at a friend's house or have the friend sleep over.
3. Going to Mc Donalds.
4. Using Dad's dartboard (with supervision).
5. Staying up an extra hour at night.

Hector's Monthly Reinforcer List

1. Collecting Hot Wheels Cars (purchase of three Hot Wheels cars).
2. Collecting Action figure (purchase of 1 action figure).

C) The mother of six-year-old Karson has made the following Reinforcer List:

Karson's Reinforcer List

1. Riding his bike - (D)
2. Going to Burger King. - (W)
3. Watching T.V. - (D)
4. Swimming. - (W)
5. Going to the park. - (W)
6. Playing with his friends in the back yard. - (D)
7. Visiting his cousin. - (W)
8. Staying the night at his friends house or having a friend sleep over. - (W)
9. Going fishing. - (M)
10. Play Station video game. - (D)
11. Spending money at the dollar store. - (W, M)
12. Get to feed the fish. - (D)

Karson's Daily Reinforcer List

1. Ride his bike.
2. Watching T.V. over 1 hour.
3. Playing at his friend's house.
4. Play Station video game.
5. Get to feed the fish.

Karson's Weekly Reinforcer List

1. Going to Burger King.
2. Go swimming.
3. Visit cousin.
4. Stay the night at friend's house or have friend sleep over.
5. Spending $2.00 at the dollar store.

Karson's Monthly Reinforcer List

1. Going fishing.
2. Spending $8.00 at the dollar store.

These are just a few examples of what your child's Reinforcer List might look like. Remember to list *only the activities and things your child likes to do or have.*

Remember that the items on your child's Reinforcer List are his **Positive Reinforcers.** These are the things you will use to give him Positive Reinforcement. As your child meets the behavioral criteria you want he earns these Positive Reinforcers. After you have made your child's Reinforcer Lists you can move on to the next step in using these Positive Reinforcers. The next step is placing these Positive Reinforcers on *Incentive Charts.* Incentive Charts are used together with the Reinforcer List for Positive Reinforcement of your child's appropriate behavior.

INCENTIVE CHARTS

The key role of the Incentive Chart is to *reinforce desired behavior <u>immediately</u> and <u>consistently</u>.* Another name for an Incentive Chart is a *Positive Reinforcer Chart.* The Incentive Chart also shows your child what is expected of him. This is done in the form of Target Behaviors (SKILLS). This will be discussed more in the chapter entitled "Target Behaviors".

The Incentive Chart combines statements of desired behavior along with the items from your child's Positive Reinforcer List. The combination of these two things works as a visual Positive Reinforcer to help teach your child new Skills (behavior) or change your child's inappropriate behavior. You can make an Incentive Chart that contains the information for just one child or you can make an Incentive Chart that contains information for many children.

The following are some examples of some Incentive Charts and an exercise designed to show you how to make and use them for your child(ren).

EXERCISE:

There are three basic kinds of Incentive Charts. They are as follows:

1. *The Daily Incentive Chart*: The Daily Incentive Chart is a chart which shows your child specific behaviors required of him during the day and specific Positive Reinforcers he can earn for meeting a specified behavior criteria.

2. *The Weekly Incentive Chart*: The Weekly Incentive Chart is a chart which shows your child that he can earn special Positive Reinforcers (once a week) by meeting his specified Daily criteria at least 4 days out of the week. It is recommended that the weekend be the time that Weekly Reinforcers are given. However, exceptions can be made if your child's schedule dictates.

3. ***The Monthly (or long term) Incentive Chart:*** The Monthly (or long term) Incentive Chart is a chart which shows your child very special Positive Reinforcers he can earn by meeting the Weekly behavior criteria at least three weeks out of the month. This Incentive Chart can be for longer than a month (such as 4-8 weeks). It is unusual to go longer than a month. It should only be done with children who are at least 10-years-old. In addition, make sure that you know the Positive Reinforcers will hold an intense value to your child for the long period. If you see it is losing its value than you may have to shorten the time. The way you will know your child is losing interest in the Reinforcer is if he shows little interest when you continually remind him of his chance to earn the Reinforcer. If he earns his Weekly Positive Reinforcer 75% of the total time of the "longer period of time" then he earns the very special Positive Reinforcer(s) at the end of the period.

Earning Reinforcers

Listed on your child's Incentive Charts are the Target Behaviors you want him to accomplish as well as a list of Positive Reinforcers he can earn for accomplishing a specific number of the Target Behaviors. The specific number of Target Behaviors he needs to accomplish for earning his Positive Reinforcers is very important. When deciding on how many Target Behaviors earn which Positive Reinforcers the basic rule to remember is; ***the greater number of Target Behaviors your child accomplishes the greater the value the Positive Reinforcers should have.*** In other words, the more Target Behaviors your child accomplishes the better the Positive Reinforcers are that he earns. Use the following criteria for specifying how many Target Behaviors your child must complete to earn his Positive Reinforcers:

Criteria for Earning Daily Positive Reinforcers: Always set your child up for success. For each number of Targeted Behaviors you have on your child's Daily Incentive Chart you need to list the specific Positive Reinforcers he can earn. These Positive Reinforcers are from your child's *Daily Reinforcer List*. The following are some examples:

A) If you have 2 Target Behaviors on your child's Daily Incentive Chart then you should have a specific Positive Reinforcer he can earn for accomplishing one Target Behavior and he should have specific Positive Reinforcers he can earn for accomplishing both of the Targeted Behaviors. Make sure that the Positive Reinforcer he earns for completing one Target Behavior has less value to him then the Positive Reinforcer he can earn for accomplishing 2 of the Target Behaviors. The best Positive Reinforcer is for the greatest number of accomplished Target Behaviors.

B) If you have 3 Target Behaviors on your child's Daily Incentive Chart then he should have a specific Positive Reinforcer he can earn for accomplishing one Target Behavior. These Positive Reinforcer (which are from his Daily Reinforcer List) will have the least value to him. The Positive Reinforcer he earns for accomplishing twoTarget Behaviors will have more value to him then the ones he earns for accomplishing just one Target Behavior. Finally, the Positive Reinforcer (from his Daily Reinforcer List) your child earns for accomplishing all three of the Target Behaviors will have the greatest value to him.

C) If your child has 4 Target Behaviors on his Daily Incentive Chart then he should have a specific Positive Reinforcer he can earn for accomplishing one Target Behavior. This Positive Reinforcer will have the least value to him. The Positive Reinforcer he earns for accomplishing two Target Behaviors is of greater value than the one he earned for one Target Behavior. The Positive Reinforcer he earns for accomplishing three Target Behaviors will have greater value than those earned for one or two Target Behaviors. Finally, the Positive Reinforcer he earns for accomplishing all four Target Behaviors will have the greatest value to him. This basic rule for increasing the value of Positive Reinforcers is used no matter how many Target Behaviors your child has for his Daily Incentive Chart.

After you have decided how many Target Behaviors your child has for the day, then take your child's Daily Reinforcer List and divide the Positive Reinforcers up by their value. Rank them according to the least valuable to the most valuable to your child.

The earning (accomplishing) of each Target Behavior on each day should be represented by a symbol such as a star, happy face, points, check mark, etc. This way your child can see his progress on the chart. This visualization of his progress also works as a Positive Reinforcer itself. As your child accomplishes his Target Behaviors have him place the star (or other symbol) on his chart.

Criteria for Earning Weekly Positive Reinforcers: Always set your child up for success. Your child will earn his Weekly Positive Reinforcers based on the number of Daily Positive Reinforcers he earned during the week. The Positive Reinforcers used for the Weekly Incentive Chart are from your child's *Weekly Reinforcer List.*

The main differences between the Daily Incentive Chart and the Weekly Incentive Chart are:

- The number of accomplished Target Behaviors needed for earning Positive Reinforcers for the Weekly Incentive Chart will be far greater than the amount of accomplished Target Behaviors needed for the Daily Incentive Chart.

- The Positive Reinforcers used for the Weekly Reinforcer List have far greater value than the Positive Reinforcers used for the Daily Reinforcer List.

- There are usually fewer Weekly Positive Reinforcers than there are Daily Positive Reinforcers. Most children won't have any more than 4 or 5 Positive Reinforcer on their Weekly Reinforcer List.

To figure out how many stars (or other symbols) your child has to earn for the Weekly Reinforcers do the following:

1. Take the total number of stars (or other symbols) he can earn for the week and Divide that number in half. If he earns half of those stars for the week then he earns 1 Weekly Reinforcer.

2. If he earns approximately 75% of his stars for the week then he earns 2 of his Weekly Reinforcers.

3. If he earns all of his stars for the week then he earns 3 of his Weekly Reinforcers. In most cases it is best not to let your child earn more than 3 Weekly Reinforcers. This keeps the value of the Weekly Reinforcers very high. Remember to make sure that Weekly Reinforcers are earned according to their value. If your child earns one Weekly Reinforcer then that Reinforcer will have the least value of the Weekly Reinforcers. If he earns 2 Weekly Reinforcers then the second one will have greater value than the first Reinforcer. If he earns all three of his Weekly Reinforcers then the third Reinforcer should have more value than the first two. By doing this your child will be motivated to earn all he can for the week.

Criteria for Earning Monthly Positive Reinforcers: Always set your child up for success. Your child will earn Monthly (or long term) Positive Reinforcers based on the number of Weekly Positive Reinforcers he earns during the month (or long term). The Positive Reinforcers used for the Monthly (or long term) Incentive Chart are from your child's *Monthly Reinforcer List.*

Most children will have 2 to 4 Monthly (or long term) Reinforcers. The Monthly Reinforcers are earned by the following criteria:

A) Take the total number of available Weekly Reinforcers your child can earn during the Month (or long term) and divide that number in half. If your child earns half of his Weekly Reinforcers available during the month (or long term) then he earns 1 of his Monthly Reinforcers.

B) If he earns approximately 75% or more of total number available then he earns 2 of his Monthly Reinforcers.

C) If your child has three Monthly Reinforcers he can earn and he earns all of the available Weekly Reinforcers during the month (or long term) then he earns all 3 of the Monthly Reinforcers. If he has 4 Monthly Reinforcers he can earn, then the maximum he should be able to earn is 3.

D) Make the first of the Monthly Reinforcers the least valuable of the Monthly Reinforcers. The second, third, and forth Monthly Reinforcers should be of equal value.

EXERCISE:

Make a practice Incentive Chart of each of the three listed above (Daily, Weekly, Monthly). The charts can be for just one child or for more than one. The following guidelines will make the process very easy:

1. The Chart should be as simple as possible.

2. It is important that the Incentive Chart is presented to your child in a positive way. For example: "Jose, you and I are going to use this Chart to help remind us of what you need to do today (this week, or this month) to earn the activities and things (Positive Reinforcers) we have put on the chart. "

3. Try to make the Incentive Chart as attractive as possible. You can use colored pens, special stickers, glitter, etc. You can also cut out different items from magazines to decorate the chart with. If at all possible, have your child do some or all of the decorating of the chart.

4. The Target Behaviors you put on the chart should be stated in the affirmative. This simply means stating in a positive way what you want your child to do, instead of what you don't want him to do.

5. The Positive Reinforcers your child can earn should be clearly written (or symbolized if your child can't read) on the chart.

6. Your child successes (accomplished Target Behaviors) should be <u>symbolized</u> by a check mark, star, happy face, sticker, etc.

7. Make sure your child understands each Target Behavior and what he has to do to accomplish that Behavior. Make sure he understands that his earning Positive Reinforcers are contingent on his accomplishing the Target Behaviors. These are done by you talking with your child each morning (and sometimes once in the evening) about the Target Behaviors he is to work on and accomplish for the day and the Positive Reinforcers he can earn. <u>Remember to encourage him. Tell him you know he can do it and you're excited to know</u>

that he is going to succeed.

8. Monitoring your child's Incentive Chart is vital to insuring success. As soon as your child completes a Target Behavior give him lots of verbal praise and have your child (if possible) put the mark of success (sticker, check, star, etc) on his chart in the appropriate place. If the Daily Incentive Chart is not reviewed daily with your child and marked then it will loose its effectiveness. This is also true of the Weekly and Monthly Incentive Charts. They must be reviewed and marked on a weekly and monthly basis. Establish a time each day when the chart is reviewed and marked. Try to choose a time when the family is together so the whole family can use this as a positive time together. If this is not possible still make the time for reviewing and marking the chart as positive as possible. REMEMBER: Consistency is the KEY! Consistency is like the wings on an airplane. If there are no wings on the plane it simply won't fly.

9. **Using School Day Schedule:** Using the "school day schedule" simply means creating an Incentive Chart and Positive Reinforcement schedule that revolves around your child's school day. This means the Positive Reinforcers he earns during his time at school he actually gets when he gets home from school.

10. **Non-School Day Schedule:** Using the "non-school day schedule" simply means creating an Incentive Chart and Positive Reinforcement schedule that revolves around non-school days. These are the days when your child is on a vacation schedule or out of school for the summer. In this type of Positive Reinforcement schedule you <u>divide your child's day in half</u>. In the morning your child can earn specific Positive Reinforcers for getting his morning chores done. The Positive Reinforcers your child earns for his Social Target Behaviors are earned by your child accomplishing those Target Behaviors for a specified period of time. For an example: John can earn "riding his bike for an hour in the afternoon" if he "keeps his hands to himself" from the time he wakes up in the morning until 1:00pm. Another example of this could be: Jennifer can earn "30 minutes of video games in the afternoon" if she talks pleasantly to her sister from the time she wakes up until 12:00 noon. The whole idea is to break your child's day up into large blocks of time in the same way "going to school" does.

You should also monitor his behavior and Incentive Chart frequently through the day. At mid-point through his day review his Charts and make available the specific Reinforcers he can earn. The Reinforcers he earns in the afternoon are based on his accomplishing the Target Behaviors in the morning.

Remember to make the least valuable Reinforcers available for the short periods of time and the most valuable Reinforcers available for the longest period of time. For an example: Tony earned 1 hour of T.V. in the afternoon because "he got his morning chores done correctly and on time". Then he earned 1 hour of video games at 4:00pm because "he completed his morning and afternoon chores completely and on time" as well as complied "immediately and pleasantly" with his mother's request from the time he got up in the morning until 4:00pm.

The following pages contain some examples of what your charts might look like:

Before you make the actual Incentive Charts that you will use with your child read chapter on Targeting Behavior and do the exercises. That chapter will show you how to decide which of your child's behaviors you want to use the Incentive Charts for. In that chapter you will also learn how to use "Cue Charts" with your Incentive Charts.

CHAPTER SUMMARY: In this chapter you have been introduced to Positive Reinforcement. Positive Reinforcement occurs when a behavior is followed by a consequence that is pleasant. There are many ways of giving Positive Reinforcement. Verbal Praise is a very powerful and effective way of using Positive Reinforcement. What you say to your child and the way you say it can have a great impact as a consequence of his behavior. Physical Affirmation is also powerful Positive Reinforcement. When you give your child a pat on the shoulder, a smile, or a hug when he is behaving appropriately you will see that appropriate behavior occur again and again. Using the Positive Reinforcer List in combination with the Incentive Chart system will enable you to create a learning and growing environment which will insure your child's success at learning new behaviors and changing inappropriate behaviors. When your child's desired activities and things (Positive Reinforcers) are contingent upon his appropriate behavior, then his behavior changes quickly and dramatically for the better. These positive quick and dramatic changes will give you Success in Parenting.

Escaping /Avoiding

Before discussing "Escaping" and "Avoiding" we must first understand what Punishment is. Punishment is simply defined as ANYTHING WHICH IS UNPLEASANT TO SOMEONE!
Punishment produces two kinds of responses: ESCAPE OR AVOIDANCE

ESCAPE: All of us have experienced situations and events in which we were so uncomfortable (Unpleasant / Punishing) that all we could think of is getting away from the situation or event. This is called ESCAPING. Let's

EXAMPLES:

A) You are sitting in a lobby of a business. A young mother is sitting next to you holding her baby. The baby begins to cry. After a while the baby's cries begin to wear on your nerves. Eventually the crying becomes so unpleasant /punishing to you that you leave the room. YOU HAVE ESCAPED THE UNPLEASANT SOUND OF THE BABY'S CRIES. THIS IS ESCAPING AN UNPLEASANT (PUNISHING) EVENT.

B) A father is shopping with his four-year-old boy. The boy begins to tantrum because his father won't buy him a candy bar. After ten minutes of the child crying the father says: "OK, here is your candy, I'll buy it for you." The boy stops crying. THE FATHER HAS ESCAPED THE BOY'S TANTRUM BY GIVING THE BOY CANDY. THIS IS ESCAPING An UNPLEASANT (PUNISHING) EVENT.

C) An Eight-year-old boy is grounded to his bedroom until he cleans his room. His friend is waiting for him to come out and play. He decides to clean his room in15 minutes to escape the unpleasant grounding.

AVOIDANCE: Once we have experienced these punishments enough times we tend to try AVOIDING them in the future. This is called AVOIDANCE. When you see an unpleasant (punishing) event or situation approaching then you try to avoid it. Let's look at some examples of avoidance:

EXAMPLES:

A) Ten-year-old John starts to run into the field barefoot. He notices large stickers up ahead of him on the ground. He stops suddenly and begins back-track out of the field where there are no stickers on the ground. JOHN HAS AVOIDED

B) THE STICKERS WHICH WOULD HAVE BEEN UNPLEASANT TO HIS FEET.

C) You're driving down the road 20 mph over the speed limit. In the distance you see a police   officer with his radar fixed on passing traffic. Upon seeing the policeman you slow down   to the posted speed limit. YOU HAVE AVOIDED A TICKET BY SLOWING DOWN.
A TICKET WOULD HAVE BEEN UNPLEASANT.

D) Eight-year-old Robert is running through the house and notices that the kitchen floor, ahead of him, has just been mopped. He stops suddenly to AVOID slipping on the wet floor. HE KNOWS TO AVOID SLIPPING AND FALLING BECAUSE IT IS
UNPLEASANT.

DESIRED RESULTS AND NEGATIVE SIDE AFFECTS

When deciding what kind of punishment to use you must consider the DESIRED RESULTS and NEGATIVE SIDE AFFECTS of the punishment. Researchers have found that punishment has its greatest effect on learning when it is used sparingly and in the mildest form necessary.

DESIRED RESULTS: The Desired Results is the desirable behavior your child displays following a punishment.

EXAMPLES:

A) Six-year-old Ryan is pushing his large toy truck through the house crashing it into the   furniture and walls. His mother ask him to stop the behavior. Ryan ignores her request   and crashes his truck into the T.V. stand. His mother then takes his truck away from him for 15 minutes. Upon getting his truck back his mother reminds him that he will lose his truck again if he crashes it into things, he finishes playing with the truck for the next hour without crashing it into anything. This is an example of "Desired Results". The   punishment here was "Loss of playing with the truck" for a period of time. When Ryan got the truck back to play with he played with it without crashing it into anything.

B) Seven-year-old Andy is standing in front of the T.V. blocking the view of his brother and   sister. His father ask him to sit in a place where everyone can see the T.V. He ignores his dad's request. His father walks over to Andy, takes him by the hand, and leads him to the "Time Out" chair. Andy is in Time Out for 3 minutes. At the end of his Time Out Andy is allowed to join the others to watch T.V. with the other children. He sits on the couch with the other children. He stays on the couch for the duration of the T.V. time. This is an example of "Desired Results". The punishment here was "Time Out". When Andy returned to the T.V. watching he sat in the appropriate place for viewing.

C) Eight-year-old Julie is playing a game. She is running through the house yelling loudly. Her mother asks her to stop the running and yelling. Julie ignores her mother's request and continues the same behavior. Mom sees that Julie has ignored her request and puts Julie in "Time Out". After Julie's Time Out she is allowed to return to playing. She is no longer running and yelling in the house. This is an example of "Desired Results".

NEGATIVE SIDE AFFECTS: Are the undesirable behaviors your child displays following a punishment. These behaviors may occur in addition to the desirable behavior.

EXAMPLES:

A) Nine-year-old Daniel is teasing his younger sister. His father punishes him by giving him 1000 sentences to write ("I will be kind to my sister"). After three hours of writing sentences Daniel stops writing and puts his head down on the table. His hand is hurting and he is overwhelmed with frustration. So far he has completed only 300 sentences. Daniel tells his dad he cannot finish the 1000 sentences because his hand hurts. His father replies "It does not matter if your hand hurts you're going to finish the sentences!" Daniel gets up from the table and runs to the bedroom crying. His dad follows him and tells him he has to stay in his room until he is ready to come out and finish the sentences. After Daniel is in his room for two hours dad goes out to mow the lawn. Daniel sneaks out of the room and goes into his sister's room. When Daniel sees that his sister is nowhere in sight he finds her favorite doll and rips the head off. He then takes another one of her favorite toys and hides it in his room. When dad comes back in from mowing the lawn Daniel tells his dad he's ready to do the sentences. Daniel then spends a couple of more hours writing sentences (he has now completed 550 sentences). Daniel's hand begins to hurt again and he tells his dad he cannot finish. Dad sends him to his room once again telling him he cannot come out until he is ready to finish the sentences. Except for dinner, Daniel stays in his room until the next day. The next day Daniel finishes up the sentences after breakfast. It takes him four hours to do so. After he finishes the punishment he is allowed to resume free play. At one point Daniel is approached by his sister to play. Daniel, still with anger towards his sister, says in a sharp tone of voice, "NO! Who would want to play with you?" Daniel ignores his sister until the following day.

This is a classic example of "Negative Side Affects". Dad's giving Daniel the sentence to write stopped Daniel from teasing his sister that day. However, dad gave Daniel too many sentences to write. As a result, we can see that Daniel engaged in breaking and hiding his sister's belongings, developing resentment towards his sister, and spending a significant amount of time in frustration and anger. The punishment was simply too much. Dad should have given Daniel about 25 sentences. This would have been reasonable for a nine-year-old (based on age). The 25 sentences would have been a short and effective appropriate punishment. Remember, punishment has its best affect if it is used sparingly and in the mildest form necessary.

B) Eleven-year-old Tammy is asked by her mother to clean up her own room. Tammy tells   her mother she does not have to clean her room because she's going over to a friend's house and doesn't have the time. Mother grabs Tammy by the hair and slaps her across   the face while yelling: You are going to clean your room or I'll knock your head off!" Tammy goes to her room crying. After cleaning her room Tammy lays on her bed feeling very depressed. Later that day Tammy goes to her friend's house and they wind up going to the mall with a group of other girls. Tammy is told by her mother to be back home by 6:00pm. As the time to go home approaches Tammy feels reluctant to go home. She feels angry at her mother and wants nothing to do with her. Tammy ends up at a friend's house instead of going home. Later that evening her mother calls over at the friend's house looking for Tammy. Tammy gets on the phone and tells her mother she's running away because her mom hit her. Her mother calls the police and the authorities end up getting involved to settle the problem.

This is another classic example of "Negative Side Affects" Tammy's mother's hitting her and yelling at her was very severe punishment. The kind of negative side effect that only produces anger, a sense of isolation, and feelings of wanting to run away. What her mother should have done was tell her she could not go to her friend's house until her room was clean and given her an extra 20 minute chore for back-talking. Corporal punishment usually produces Undesirable Side Affects and has been shown in thousands of studies, world-wide, to be the least desirable method for changing behavior.

C) Five-year-old Megan is jumping on the couch. Mother asks Megan to stop the jumping on the couch and go play in her own room. Megan ignores her mother's request. Mother then grounds Megan to her room for a week. By the end of the day Megan is sitting on her bed crying because she can't leave her room to play with the other children. Except for meals and bathing, Megan spends her days in her room by herself. After the third day Megan becomes very frustrated and cries periodically. By the fourth day Megan is displaying outburst of anger and starting to break some of her toys. By the fifth day she begins wetting her pants slightly and telling her mom, "I just couldn't hold it."

By the sixth day Megan's mom decides to let her come out of her room. In the weeks following Megan has "slightly wet-pants" several times a day. She tells her mom she can't make it to the bathroom on time.

This is another classic example of Negative Side Effects. The punishment of being grounded to the bedroom for a week was too overwhelming for Megan. The Undesirable Side Affects of crying spells, frequent outburst of anger, breaking toys, and wetting her pants are all caused by too severe of punishment. It is important to note that: As the severity of a punishment increases so does the anxiety level. The more anxiety a child experiences from the punishment the more Undesirable Side Affects will occur.

CHOOSING PUNISHMENTS (NEGATIVE CONSEQUENCES)

The GOAL in using effective punishment is to "INTERRUPT, STOP, OR DECREASE INAPPROPRIATE BEHAVIOR". There is a wide range of punishments people use to "Interrupt, Stop, or Decrease inappropriate behavior". In this book we are going to discuss the punishments which Behavioral Psychologists have discovered to be most effective in Interrupting, Stopping, or Decreasing inappropriate behavior. These are punishments, which if used correctly, produce the least amount of "Negative Side Affects".

Another term for punishment is **NEGATIVE CONSEQUENCE**. The following list of Punishments / Negative Consequences are those which have been proven to work the best in changing behavior. Punishments / Negative Consequences work best sparingly and in the mildest form necessary and should always be used in conjunction with Positive Reinforcement. This will insure "Desired Results".

NEGATIVE CONSEQUENCES

There are many kinds of effective punishments that can be implemented to change behavior. The following are the most effective:

1. **Time Out**: One of the most effective kinds of punishment you can use is Time Out. However, Time Out is one of the most misunderstood and misused punishments that is being used today. It is important to use Time Out properly, or it won't be effective. Behavioral Psychologists have spent years perfecting this technique. We will not endeavor to go into all the many clinical principles of giving a Time Out. However, we have simplified it into an easy-to-follow

form.

Time Out is a mild, but effective, punishment that consists of the following GUIDELINES and STEPS:

GUIDELINES: Make sure you follow these guidelines when using
Time Out to punish your child:

A) The child should sit on a chair or stand in a particular spot. It is usually best to use a chair, but if none are available the child may stand. If the environment is appropriate he can also sit on the floor. Never put a child in a corner, it can damage their vision You can use a particular room for Time Out as long as there is a designated place to sit in that room.

B) The Time Out should be *two minutes* long for children 4-9 years of age and three to *five minutes* long for children 10-12 years-of-age.

C) The Time Out should be away from all activities. Such as an area of the room where there is no play or other people. The goal is to separate the child from activity.

D) When you place your child in Time Out tell him what INAPPROPRIATE BEHAVIOR(S) he is going to Time Out for.

E) While your child is in Time Out he should not engage in ANY activity (this includes talking). Your child should remain quiet and calm for the duration of the Time Out.

F) If he begins to talk or engage in some kind of play activity during the Time Out, the Time Out starts over.

G) If your child begins to back talk during you're placing him in Time Out or during his doing the Time Out, then he is not ready for Time Out. Many parents complain that they put their child in Time Out and their child just continues to "act-out". This is because the child is NOT READY for Time Out. If your child is not ready for Time Out he should be sent to his room until he is ready to take his Time Out in a pleasant manner. Sometimes your child will not be ready for Time Out for a long while. Sometimes it could take as much as an hour before he is ready. He will eventually be ready.

H) At the end of the Time Out ask your child to tell you what INAPPROPRIATE BEHAVIOR he was sent to Time Out for. Within about 30 seconds your child should begin to tell you the specific behavior he was sent to Time Out for. Basically, he will just repeat to you what you stated when you sent him to Time

48

Out.   After he has told you the inappropriate behavior he was sent to Time Out for, then he needs to tell you the appropriate behavior he should have been doing. In the beginning you will most likely have to give him suggestions as to the appropriate behavior. After a number of Time Outs he will get the idea and be able to state the appropriate behavior on his own. This action of your child stating what he should have been doing will send your child away from the Time Out thinking about the appropriate behavior.

STEPS: Make sure you follow these **STEPS** when you use Time Out to punish your child:

A) When you see your child engaged in an inappropriate behavior and you decide he should be put in Time Out, take action immediately. Don't give them multiple warnings! A simple rule to remember is: ONLY TELL YOUR CHILD TO STOP

THE INAPPROPRIATE BEHAVIOR ONE TIME. IF HE DOSE NOT STOP IMMEDIATELY THEN PUT HIM IN TIME OUT. If you apply this rule your child   soon learns that you mean what you say the FIRST time you say it, not the fifth or sixth.

B) Taking Action: Tell your child to go to Time Out for (inappropriate behavior). Give him a very brief description of the inappropriate behavior.

EXAMPLES:

1. "John, go to Time Out for hitting your sister."
2. "Kathy, take a Time Out for not accepting my decision."
3. "Mike, take a Time Out for back-talking me."
4. "Timmy, go to Time out for throwing the ball in the house."
5. "Rosie, take a Time Out for playing with your sister's doll without permission."
6. "Karen, go to Time Out for jumping on the furniture."
7. "Jesse, take a Time Out for yelling in the house."

Remember: Your child needs to know exactly what behavior he is doing wrong. Never use generalized statements like: "go to Time Out for being bad, or go to Time Out for misbehaving." These types of statements are vague at best. They do not convey to your child the proper information about the inappropriate behavior.

C) Within about 30 seconds your child should go to the Time Out place (chair, spot). If they don't go to Time Out immediately and pleasantly then they are not ready for the Time Out. Send them to their room until they are ready to take their Time Out.   Sometimes this will take a few minutes and other times in can take an hour.

D) Observe your child in the Time Out to make sure they are doing the Time Out properly. Remember, no activity.

E) At the end of the Time Out ask your child what behavior he was sent to Time Out for. He should tell you the inappropriate behavior he was sent to Time Out for. Sometimes your child may not respond to your question within an appropriate amount of time (60 seconds). At this point remind him what he was sent to Time Out for and give him EXTRA TIME (the same amount of time of his regular Time Out). After the time is up repeat the process of asking him why he was sent to Time Out and why he got extra time. If he still is not ready to respond to your question in an appropriate manner then send him to his room until he is ready to take his Time Out properly. When he is ready to come out of his room then the Time Out process starts over. This may sound like a lot of time and effort. However, it actually takes very little effort and the time goes by very quickly. If your child has to go to his room a few times before he does Time Out appropriately, then he learns quickly that not taking his Time Out in a pleasant manner does not pay off for him. He will soon adjust to doing his Time Out pleasantly.

F) After he tells you what he was sent to Time Out for, then ask him what appropriate behavior he should have been doing. You may have to give him suggestions in the beginning, but he will soon catch on to thinking about and stating what he should have been doing.

EXAMPLES:

A) Six-year-old Justin is teasing his younger sister as she watches T.V. His dad asks him to stop the teasing behavior. He ignores his father's request and continues. His dad tells him to go to Time Out for "Teasing his sister". Justin goes over to the "Time Out chair" (a designated kitchen chair placed away from the kitchen table) and sits down quietly in a pleasant manner to take his time out. After two minutes his dad says to him: "Justin, how come you were sent to Time Out?" Justin replies: "Because I was teasing my sister." His dad asks: "What should you have been doing?" Justin replies: "Watching T.V. quietly." Dad then tells him: "Justin, you can go back and watch T.V. quietly."

B) Eight-year-old Kristy ask her mom if she can go outside to play. Her mom tells her it is almost time for dinner and she needs to stay inside. Kristy does not like her mom's decision and starts to argue with her mother. After Kristy's first arguing statement her mother tells her to take a Time Out for not accepting her decision. Kristy goes to the Time Out chair (a designated kitchen chair placed away from the kitchen table) and takes her Time Out in a pleasant manner. After two minutes Kristy's mom asks her: "Kristy, why were you sent to Time

Out?" Kristy replies: "I did not accept your decision, I was arguing with you." Kristy's mother then asks her: "What should you do when I make a decision?" Kristy responded: "I should accept your decision pleasantly."

C) Ten-year-old Allen is running through the house and jumping on the furniture. His mother tells him to stop. He ignores her request. His mother tells him to take a Time Out for running through the house and jumping on the furniture. Allen stops what he is doing and goes to the Time Out chair and sits down. He pulls a small toy from his pocket and begins to play with it. His mother reminds him that there is no playing in Time Out and tells him to put the toy away. He complies. About 30 seconds later Allen takes the toy out and begins to play with it again. Allen's mother tells him to go to his room until he is ready for Time Out. Allen goes to his room. After 5 minutes his mother asks him if he is ready for his Time Out. He tells her he is ready. His mother then asks him how he is supposed to take his Time Out. He replies, "quietly and without playing." Allen's mother then tells him he can go to the Time Out chair and take his Time Out. After taking his Time Out properly his mother asks him what he was sent to Time Out for. He replies: "I was running through the house and jumping on the furniture." His mother then asks him, "Where are you supposed to run and jump Allen?" He replies: "Outside of the house." After his correct response his mother then allows him to leave Time Out.

EXERCISE FOR TIME OUT:

1. Role-play using Time Out with another adult. Do at least twenty role plays. Switch back and forth from playing the adult role to playing the child role.

2. Use all the Guidelines and Steps mentioned above.

3. After each role play discuss (with your role play partner) how well you implemented each Guideline and each Step mentioned above. Be open to constructive observation by your partner. Discuss what you did correctly in giving the Time Out. If you did something wrong then discuss with your partner how you could have better followed the Guidelines and Steps in implementing the Time Out. Try to implement changes in the next role play that will enable you to follow the Guidelines and Steps as close as possible.

A) Grounding: Grounding consists of restricting your child to his room, house, yard, or any specific area which has boundaries. There is also a specific time period for grounding. Your child's age and the type of inappropriate behavior he did will dictate the location where he is grounded and the time period for which he is grounded. The following are a few simple guidelines to remember when grounding your child:

B) Remember: Grounding is not Time Out. Grounding involves your child being able to do some kind of activity in a limited area. Time Out involves your child doing NO activity.

C) The longer a child is grounded the less desired effect the grounding has. It is better to ground your child for an hour, or a few hours, a day, or a few days.

D) Avoid Grounding your child for weeks on end. A long Grounding period significantly reduces your ability to effectively use the Incentive Chart system and reduces the effects of Positive Reinforcement.

E) While your child is grounded it may affect his ability to earn certain Positive Reinforcers. These are the Positive Reinforcers that involve his going beyond the limits of the grounding. For Example: Jose has a Positive Reinforcer of being able to Play Nintendo. The Nintendo is located in the living room. If he is grounded to his room then he unavailable for that particular Positive Reinforcer. It is appropriate for your child to have access to limited (small) Positive Reinforcers while being grounded for a long period (1 day or more).

2. **Loss of Privilege**: Loss of Privilege involves loss of the opportunity to do some activity or have a particular thing. It can involve loss of an immediate privilege or thing or a loss of a privilege or thing in the near future. The follow are some guidelines to remember when taking away your child's privileges:

A) The loss of privilege should be kept to a minimum. Your child can either loose the privilege of the activity he is currently doing, or one or two privileges in the near future.

B) The more privileges you take away the less Positive Reinforcers you can give your child for appropriate behavior. Remember, your child's privileges are his Positive Reinforcers. Make sure you limit the loss of privilege.

C) If your child makes you angry by his inappropriate behavior wait until you cool off before you remove his privileges (Positive Reinforcers). Remember, your own anger can sabotage your efforts in teaching your child.

D) Make sure that you don't take away a privilege (Positive Reinforcer) that your child has been working towards earning for a long period of time. For example: If Tina has been doing well all week and acts out just before she is to get her Weekly Reinforcer, than don't take away the Weekly Reinforcer. Instead take away a smaller Reinforcer or use another type of punishment. The Weekly and

Monthly Positive Reinforcers represent how your child has done all week or all month. The Loss of Privilege should represent the short period of time for the acting out.

3. **Writing Sentences**: Writing Sentences consist of your child writing a number of sentences which state "what he should have done". These are some guidelines to remember when giving your child sentences write for punishment:

A) Make sure the sentence is in Affirmative form. This way your child is writing about what he should have done, instead of what wrong he did. Here are some examples:

- "I will accept my mom's decisions" (instead of, "I will not talk back").
- "I will cooperate with my dad" (instead of, "I will not refuse to do my chore").
- "I will call my brother by his name" (instead of, "I will not call my brother names").

➢ The goal is to get your child to write what he "will do", instead of what he "will not do".

B) Make the amount of sentences in groups of 5, 10, or 25. For the younger child who writes slower make sure you don't give him over 15-20 sentences. You should design the punishment to last anywhere from 10 minutes (for a minor inappropriate behavior) to 1 hour (for major inappropriate behavior).

C) Avoid giving large amounts of sentences to write. It is easy to get angry and tell your child he has to write 500 or 5,000 sentences. This is ineffective. This usually takes a lot of time and keeps your child in a negative consequences too long. The longer he is in the negative consequence the longer he is unavailable to be Positively Reinforced for appropriate behavior. If you feel like you have to give him a more severe punishment then consider a combination of two punishments (instead of the 5,000 sentences).

4. **Extra Jobs (Chores):** Giving your child Extra Jobs or Chores for a punishment consist of giving him a 10 to 30 minute job that is not one of his usual responsibilities. This works best with children who are eight-years-old or older. It is not to effective with children younger than this. The following are some examples and guidelines for this kind of punishment.

- Sweep the porch.
- Fold laundry.
- Rake leaves.

- Pull weeds.
- Shovel snow.
- Load the dishwasher.

- Mop the floor.	- Vacuum the den.
- Clean out the car.	- Organize the video shelf.
- Wash down kitchen cabinets	- Match and fold Socks.
- Wash out the bathtub.	- Wash the car.
- Dust furniture.	- Sweep the driveway.

These are just a few examples. You may or may not want your child to use the extra jobs that are on this list. If not, then just look around your house and think of simple jobs that take 10-30 minutes to do. Depending on the age of your child and the seriousness of his inappropriate behavior you can give him more than one extra job at a time. Just remember, the longer he is in a negative consequence the less time he has to be Positively Reinforced for appropriate behavior. Try to limit the Extra Jobs to no more than 3 (maximum) in one punishment situation.

Follow these guidelines when giving this kind of punishment:

A) Make sure the job you're wanting to your child to do is developmentally appropriate. Make sure you know he has all the skills necessary to do the work.

B) Make sure he is not doing one of his regular chores.

C) Make sure he is not doing another child's regular chore. It is important that the other child not lose his responsibilities so his sibling can be punished.

If you feel you need to give your child more than three Extra Jobs for his inappropriate behavior than you can add on a very short grounding and a small amount of sentences to write. Of course, this would be for very serious inappropriate behavior. If your child has made you angry by what he did remember: Keep your anger out of your child's learning experience. The goal is to teach, not vent your anger.

5. **Subject Writing Exercise**: This punishment consist of giving your child a short writing exercise on the subject of why he is being punished. This can only work with older children. This works best with children who are ten-years-old or older. It is only effective if your child has enough writing skills to complete the exercise. The following are some simple guidelines for   making this punishment effective:

A) Have your child write about one page on how he should have done things differently in the situation. If your child has a creative bent then he can sometimes write two full pages. Most kids can only do about one page.

B) You will need to give your child suggestions on how to write what you want.

Discuss in detail what you want him to think about and write about.

C) The basic content of the assignment should include what he did wrong and appropriate alternative ways of handling the situation differently. He should write about positive ways to have handled things differently.

6. **Restitution**: This punishment involves your child restoring something that he destroyed or lost. This punishment works well if it is within your child's ability to do this. If he can't make full Restitution (such as paying for a window he broke) then he can make Partial Restitution. If your child is earning money as part of his Positive Reinforcers than don't use this money to pay for Restitution. Create extra jobs he can do to earn the money for Restitution.

Guidelines for Giving Punishment

1. Keep your number one goal that of Interrupting / Stopping or Decreasing your child's inappropriate.

2. Use the mildest form of punishment possible.

3. Increase the level of punishment slowly.

4. When you use punishment make sure you also Positively Reinforce the behavior that is incompatible with the inappropriate behavior.

EXAMPLES:

A) If you are going to punish your child for back talk then make sure you give him lots of Positive Reinforcement (such as verbal praise) each time he accepts your decision pleasantly.

B) If you are going to punish your child for yelling in the house then give him lots of Positive Reinforcement (such as verbal praise) when he is talking quietly or within an acceptable level.

C) If you're going to punish your child for hitting his sister in a conflict then give him lots of Positive Reinforcement (such as verbal praise) when he attempts to resolve his conflicts in an appropriate verbal manner.

5. When you give your child a punishment then don't back out of it. If you do then you will destroy the learning experience.

6. If you give a punishment that is too severe then the punishment can be changed as soon as you realize that it is too severe. When this happens let your child know you have given him too severe of a punishment. Don't back out of punishing him, just change the punishment to a punishment which has Desired Side Affects.

7. **Don't punish out of anger**. Take the time to cool off so you can give a punishment that is based on the inappropriate behavior, not your own anger.

8. **Post a chart of "Negative Consequences"** where your child can read it. If your child can't read then use symbols on the chart to represent each punishment. If a chart of "Negative Consequences" is where your child can see it and be reminded of it often then he can see the consequences of inappropriate behavior in advance.

9. Make sure that all of the "adults-in-charge" (those who have the authority to give the punishment) stick to the chart of "Negative Consequences". If they don't then your child's learning experience will be sabotaged.

10. Make sure that all of the "adults-in-charge" agree with these Guidelines and can flow with your decisions about the punishments you want your child to receive. If they don't then your child's learning experience will be sabotaged.

11. **Avoid using your voice as punishment** (yelling and screaming at your child). Over time this causes an assortment of problems with your child. It can also make you upset as well as potentially sabotage your efforts to have a healthy parent-child relationship.

12. If your child is being given punishments frequently then there is a problem. If this becomes a problem for your child you need to re-examine how often and what kind of Positive Reinforcement you are giving him for appropriate behavior. Children cannot thrive and be emotionally health in Punishment Based Environments (Environments that predominately use punishment to change and motivate behavior).

13. **Post a Negative Consequences Chart**: Post a Chart of Negative Consequences your child can receive for his inappropriate behavior. It should be in a place where your child can view it easily. If your child can't read then you can use symbols on the list. Don't make the chart large and attractive. It should be very simple and plain. We suggest that you place on the list the punishments we have in this book. The goal is to make your child aware of the Negative Consequences of his inappropriate behavior and be able to understand, as much as possible the potential consequences of his inappropriate

behavior before he does it.   On the following   page is a sample "Negative Consequences Chart":

Temper Tantrums

Temper Tantrums may occur when your are attempting to use some kind of punishment method with your child or they may occur when your child doesn't get his way about something.   Generally, Temper Tantrums must be treated like any other kind of inappropriate behavior. However, there are some things that you need to know about "Real Temper Tantrums".   A good understanding of the real nature of Tantrums will help you better cope with your child when he is having one and better equip you to change this kind of behavior. Most children experience two basic kinds of Temper Tantrums. The first kind is a mild one in which a child goes into a "Mild Fit of Rage" because he doesn't get his way about something. The second kind is when a child goes into a "Deep Fit of Rage" because he didn't get his way about something.

There are two things that children experience in both kinds of Tantrums: 1) Anger, and 2) A loss of self-control. The only thing that distinguishes the "Mild Fit of Rage" from the "Deep Fit of Rage" is the intensity a child experiences with his anger and loss of self-control .

When a child is having a "Mild Tantrum" then he should be sent to his room until he gains enough self-control to come out of his room and receive his punishment. Don't be worried about how long it takes him to gain self-control. For some children it will take five minutes and for some it could take an hour, even longer. Make sure he receives some sort of punishment (one of the ones recommended in this book). His punishment doesn't start until he is calm. When you tell him what his punishment is and he starts to tantrum again then begin the process over again. If he begins to tantrum at any stage of his punishment then the process starts all over again. If you are out in public when he starts this kind of Tantrum then let him know you will take him home immediately or take him to the car or to some place where he will have to sit in Time Out or receive some other kind of punishment. If he follows through with his Tantrum then follow through with what you have told him you will do.

The only time you should consider not punishing your child for a Tantrum or consider using a very mild punishment for a Tantrum is if there are stress factors contributing or causing the Tantrum. It is important to recognize that certain stress factors can contribute greatly to tantrums.   There are some common ones you should be aware of.   One stress factor that is common with many children in some situations is a low blood sugar. If your child is experiencing a low blood sugar (being hungry) then his ability to cope with stress is much lower and he may be more vulnerable to tantrum. Make sure this is not the case for your child. If your child has gone more than two to three hours between meals or snacks he may have a low blood sugar. Of course younger children are more vulnerable to this than older children. Another stress factor that affects children's ability to cope with stress is "being tired". When your child is tired his ability to cope with stress can plummet. Make sure your child is getting enough rest. Sometimes a child is exposed to an unjust or unfair situation which is far to overwhelming him to cope with (such as being severely teased by an older child). Make sure you try to keep your child from this kind of vulnerability.

When your child begins to Tantrum you should immediately ask yourself if any of these factors are contributing to your child's Tantrum. If they are you should remedy the mitigating factor(s) immediately.

When your child is in the "Deep Fit of Rage" kind of Tantrum then you need to recognize that he is very angry and, most important, that he has lost all control of himself . Your first goal in this situation is to make sure that he does not hurt himself or others. He must be removed from the opportunity to do either. He should be sent to his room. You may have to mildly restrain him or physically assist him to his room. Do not escalate the situation by becoming angry and throwing a fit yourself. Remain calm. The procedure for this kind of Tantrum is similar to the procedure for the Mild Tantrum. Find a place for your child to be alone. His bedroom usually works well. If you are at the store you can use your car. However, if your child goes to the car to calm down then you should stay with him. Never leave an "out-of-control" child in a car by himself. If you are visiting at someone's home then they might lend a room to you for your child to "cool off" in. Again, the main goal in this kind of Tantrum is to get your child completely calmed down so that you can issue an appropriate punishment.

CHAPTER SUMMARY*: Punishment produces two kinds of responses, Escape or Avoidance. It is important to understand how punishment impact's your child. Your ability to punish your child and get the "Desired Side Affects" is crucial to your child's learning experience in life and his mental health. When you use the punishments that produce the "Desired Side Affects" you stop or weaken an undesirable behavior without creating excessive anxiety in your child. The more anxiety your child has the more he will "act out". Remember that severe or overwhelming punishments are the ones that create the excessive anxiety and Negative Side Affects. If you implement punishments that stop or weaken inappropriate behavior with no Negative Side Affects you will have Success in Parenting.*

Targeting Behavior

Targeting Behavior simply means *Pin Pointing* or identifying particular behaviors you want your child to change or learn. Two ways of Targeting (Pin Pointing) Behavior are:

1. Pin pointing **Behavior Excess**. A **Behavior Excess** is an inappropriate or unpleasant behavior which you do not want your child to engage in.

OR

2. Pin Pointing a **Behavior Deficit**. A **Behavior Deficit** is a desired appropriate behavior you want your child to engage in that he is doing very little of or not at all. In this book we are going to call this desired appropriate behavior a **Skill**. A **Skill** is an ability to perform a certain task.

TARGETING (PIN-POINTING) BEHAVIOR EXCESSES

As we stated above, Behavior Excess is an inappropriate or unpleasant behavior that you <u>do not</u> want your child engaging in. The way to identify Behavior Excess is through observation. Sometimes the behavior Excess will be very obvious; such as hitting, kicking, breaking things, screaming, tantrums, etc. There are other times when you will need to observe your child and write your observation down (as discussed in chapter entitled "What is Behavior?). Written observations are a great resource for pin-pointing behaviors.

There are two ways to change Behavior Excesses (Inappropriate Behavior):

1. <u>Ignore the inappropriate behavior</u> and Positively Reinforce an appropriate behavior that is incompatible with the inappropriate behavior. The following are some examples:

    A) Seven-year-old Jeremy and his mother are shopping. He asks his mother to buy him a candy bar. His mother tells him no. He continues to ask her repeatedly over a ten minute period. Jeremy's mother ignores his continued request. Twenty minutes later Jeremy is walking quietly next to his mother as she shops. Suddenly his mother stops, smiles at him and says, "Jeremy, I sure like the way you are staying next to me and being so patient while I shop". In this situation Jeremy's inappropriate behavior was <u>repeatedly asking his</u>

B) mother for a candy bar after she had told him no. His mother ignores his repeated request. Ten minutes after he stops making the requests he is behaving appropriately. At this point his mother gives him verbal Positive Reinforcement for his appropriate behavior. In this situation Jeremy's appropriate behavior of walking quietly next to his mother (for ten minutes) while she shops was incompatible with making repeated request for candy. His mother has Positively Reinforced the appropriate incompatible behavior.

C) Five-year-old Billy is making annoying verbal noises in the back seat of the car as his mother drives down the road. He does this off and on for almost fifteen minutes. His mother ignores his noise making. After he stops making then annoying noises he sits ridding quietly for ten minutes. Suddenly his mother smiles and blurts out, "Billy you are so quiet, that is so nice, you make mommy so happy when you are quiet when I am driving, you are such a great helper!".

In this situation Billy's inappropriate behavior was making noises in the back seat while his mother was driving the car. His mother ignores his inappropriate behavior of "making noises". After Billy has been sitting and riding quietly for ten minutes his mother gives him verbal Positive Reinforcement for his appropriate behavior. His sitting and riding quietly is incompatible with him making verbal noises. His mother ignored the inappropriate behavior and Positively Reinforced the appropriate behavior. Billy's appropriate behavior of riding quietly was incompatible with his inappropriate behavior of making noises.

D) Twelve-year-old Sarah asks her father if she can go to the show alone on Friday night. Her father tells her no. Sarah continues to whine to her father about going for over an hour. Her father ignores her whining. An hour after she stops whining her father notices that she is sitting quietly and doing her homework. He walks over to her and gives her a hug and tells her, "I can see you're working hard at getting your home work done every night. It really makes me proud to have a daughter who does so well in school!"

In this situation Sarah's inappropriate behavior was whining. Her father ignores the "whining" behavior. An hour after Sarah has stopped whining her father notices that she is sitting quietly and doing her homework. Her father then gives her verbal and physical Positive Reinforcement for the appropriate behavior of sitting quietly and doing homework. Sarah's behavior of sitting quietly and doing her homework is incompatible with whining. Her father ignored the inappropriate behavior and Positively Reinforced the appropriate behavior.

2. <u>Punish the inappropriate behavior</u> and Positively Reinforce the appropriate behavior which is incompatible with the inappropriate behavior. The following are some examples:

    A) Six-year-old Juan is <u>jumping on the couch</u>. His mother ask him to stop and he ignores her. <u>Jaun's mother then puts him in Time Out</u> for his inappropriate behavior of jumping on the couch. After Juan's Time Out he sits on the floor and calmly plays with his legos. After he has been playing appropriately for ten minutes his mother says to him, "Juan, I sure like the way you are sitting on the floor playing with your legos. You are following the house rules really well".

    In this situation Jaun's inappropriate behaviors were <u>jumping on the couch and ignoring his mother's request that he stop</u>. His mother punishes him by giving him a <u>Time Out.</u> After the Time Out Juan begins to play appropriately. After ten minutes of his playing appropriately his mother gives him verbal Positive Reinforcement. His appropriate behavior of playing calmly was incompatible with jumping on the couch. After Juan had been punished for his inappropriate behavior he was then Positively Reinforced for an appropriate behavior which was incompatible with the inappropriate behavior.

    B) Nine-year-old Erik is calling his sister names. His father tells him to stop. Erik ignores his father's request and continues to call her names. Erik's father then give's Erik twenty sentencing to write: "I will call my sister by her real name". After Erik finishes his sentences he starts to play video games with his sister and talk with her about school. After ten minutes of his playing appropriately and talking appropriately with his sister Erik's father approaches him, pats him on the shoulder, smiles, and says, "Erik, I like the way you are talking to your sister."

    In this situation Erik's inappropriate behaviors were <u>calling his sister names and ignoring his father's request that he stop.</u> His father gives him a <u>punishment of twenty sentences to write.</u> After Erik completes his punishment he starts to play and talk with his sister appropriately. Ten minutes into his playing and talking appropriately with his sister his father gives him verbal and physical Positive Reinforcement for the appropriate behavior. After Erik's father punished his inappropriate behavior he then took the opportunity to Positively Reinforce his appropriate behavior. Erik's behavior of playing and talking to his sister appropriately was incompatible with calling his sister names.

C) Eleven-year-old Tracy is asked by her mother to help put some groceries away in the kitchen. Tracy refuses to help and tells her mother that she doesn't have to help because she did it last time and it is her older brother's turn to help put the groceries away. Tracy's mother gives Tracy a punishment of an extra chore of scrubbing out the kitchen sink (a 5 minute job) for refusing to help and back- talk. In addition to this Tracy had to help put away the groceries. One hour later Tracy's mother asks her to set the table for dinner. Tracy complies with her mother's request immediately and cheerfully. After two minutes of Tracy staying on task her mother approaches her with a big smile and says, "Tracy, you are such a great helper, I am going to let you chat with your friends online for an extra hour today". Tracy is very excited by the extra privilege.

In this situation Tracy's inappropriate behaviors were <u>refusing to help</u> her mother and back-talking her mother. Her mother gives her a <u>punishment of an extra chore.</u> One hour later Tracy's mother asks her to set the table. After two minutes of Tracy staying on task her mother approaches her and gives her verbal praise and an extra privilege. These two things are Positive Reinforcement for her appropriate behavior. In this situation Tracy's mother punished the inappropriate behavior and Positively Reinforced the appropriate behavior.

A more comprehensive list of effective punishments and guidelines to their use is found in chapter entitled Escape and Avoidance.

Index of Behavior Excesses

The following is a quick reference index to help you identify Behavior Excesses more efficiently:

Inappropriate Play: This occurs when your child does not play with toys or game appropriately or does not follow the rules of the game.

Dawdling: This consists of your child using an excessive amount of time to do a task because he is engaging in behaviors he is not supposed to.

Whining: This behavior consists of your child continuously complaining in a tiresome way.

Back-talk: This consists of your child inappropriately questioning your decision or request. It involves your child's attempts to carry on the discussion after you have made a decision. It is also defined as inappropriate physical gestures your child makes after you have made a decision.

Arguing: This behavior consists of aggressive verbal debates with siblings or other children.

Noisy: This behavior consists of making excessively loud or frequent noise. It includes behaviors such as, screaming, shouting, banging, whistling, etc.

Physical Aggression: This behavior consist of hostile physical behavior directed towards another person. It can also include physical gestures or verbal threats that involve violence.

Overreacting: This behavior consists of an exaggerated or over-dramatized response to a situation. It is usually accompanied with fast speech or jumping up and down or yelling.

Non-Compliance: This behavior consists of your child failing to comply with your request. It also includes your child verbally complying but not completing the task you requested.

Silly: This behavior consists of excessive giggling or laughter in an inappropriate setting.

Not Minding One's Own Business: This behavior consist of your child interfering in the affairs of someone else when he is not directly involved in the activity. This includes your child attempting to participate in your correction of another child.

Physical Destructiveness: This consists of rough or damaging treatment of toys or other property.

Teasing: This behavior consists of behaviors that include annoying, mocking, pestering, or harassing another person is such a way that the other person will show displeasure or disapproval. This includes physical gestures that can produce the same affect.

Tantrum: This behavior consists of your child acting out in a fit of rage. This includes physical and verbal fits of rage.

Stealing: This consists of your child taking and / or possessing something that does not belong to him.

Inappropriate Location: This behavior consists of your child being in an area which he is not allowed to be with the permission of the person in-charge of that area (such as in a sibling's room or dad's garage).

This index is in no way a complete list of Behavior Excesses. However, it can act as a quick reference or basic list to help you identify some of the most common Behavior Excesses.

TARGETING (PIN-POINTING) BEHAVIOR DEFICITS

As we stated above, a Behavior Deficit is a *Desired Appropriate Behavior* that occurs very little or not at all. In this book we are terming the Desired Appropriate Behavior a **SKILL**. A SKILL is an ability to perform a specific task.

In this book we have listed Skill Areas for Pin Pointing (Targeting) Behavior Deficits:

PERSONAL SKILLS: These Skills involve your child's care and control of his personal property and space. This also includes self-hygiene. The following are some examples:

- Cleaning bedroom.
- Getting dressed.
- Brushing teeth.
- Picking up one's own toys.
- Cleaning up after self in bathroom.
- Combing hair.

HOUSEHOLD SKILLS: These Skills related to general housekeeping.
The following are some examples:

- Folding laundry (if old enough).
- Vacuuming (if old enough).
- Yard work (if old enough).
- Putting the dishes away.
- Taking out the trash.
- Washing dishes.
- Cleaning living room.
- Sweeping the floor.

EDUCATIONAL SKILLS: These Skills are related to your child's education. You can choose to either use a "School Card" system with your child or just make this part of your child's daily Target Behaviors without the School Card. However, if your child is having struggles at school it is recommended that you use the "School Card" system. The following are some examples:

- Getting to school on time.
- Working quietly at desk.
- Turning homework in.

- Completing homework.
- Following directions.
- Raise hand to talk.

SOCIAL SKILLS: These Skills refer to your child's social behavior, both at home and out in public. The following are some examples:

- Asking "please".
- Speaking pleasantly to others.
- Sharing belongings.
- Speaking politely.
- Accepting decisions.

- Co-operating with siblings.
- Immediate pleasant compliance.
- Asking to use other's possessions.
- Following Directions.
- Keep hands to self.

Now that we know about Skills lets take a look at some effective ways you can teach these Skills to your child. In this book we will show you two very effective methods which utilize Stating Behavioral Expectations and Positive Reinforcement to teach Skills to your child. These two methods are **Incentive Charts** and **Cue Charts.** Incentive Charts are basically *Positive Reinforcer* charts and Cue Charts are basically *Reminder* charts.

INCENTIVE CHARTS: The primary role of the Incentive Chart is to Positively Reinforce specific Skills immediately and consistently. The Incentive Chart combines statements about specific Skills you want your child to learn along with a list of Positive Reinforcers your child can earn for his performance in the specific Skills Areas. The design and use of Incentive Charts is detailed in chapter entitled "Positive Reinforcement".

CUE CHARTS: Cue Charts are basically attractive signs which tell and *Remind* your child WHAT behaviors are expected of him. These charts are crucial for letting your child know *what* behaviors are expected of him, *when* he is to do these behaviors, *where* he is to do these behaviors, and *how* he is to do these behaviors. Cue Charts are posted in an areas or places which will best guarantee your child will see them. The following are some examples: Kitchen (for "Cleaning the Kitchen" chart), Bathroom (for "Cleaning the Bathroom" or "Taking A Bath" chart), Bedroom (for "Bedroom Chores" chart), etc.

The main differences between the Cue Charts and the Incentive Charts are that the Cue Charts are usually multiple and they list many more Skills than are listed on the Incentive Chart. There are usually many Cue Charts throughout the house. The Cue Charts can be for each area of the house. The Cue Charts give details about many different Skills. There are usually only two or three Incentive Charts for each child and each Incentive Chart has only a small number of specific Skills. Another difference between the two is the Cue Chart does not list any Positive Reinforcers on it. The primary role of the Incentive Chart is *to give Positive Reinforcement* and the primary role of the Cue Chart is *to give Reminders*.

In designing Cue Charts you must use the following Guidelines:

1. Describe in short specific terms what behavior you want your child to do. The following are some examples: "Put dirty clothes in laundry basket", "Hang up jacket", "Vacuum living room", "Put dishes in sink after dinner", etc. If your child can read then use the language suited for their reading level. If the chart is for multiple children who are at different reading levels (Ex: ages 5-10) then use language for the lowest reading level. If the chart includes children who can read as well as those who can't read, then use pictures alongside of the sentence describing the task.

2. The behavior must be stated in the Affirmative form. For example: "Fold clothes and put them in your dresser", rather than: "Do not leave your clothes on the floor".

3. List as few steps as possible. For example: If you were making one for "Bathing", your chart might include the following steps:

    1. Take off clothes and put them in the laundry hamper.
    2. Take a bath/shower.
    3. Hang up washrag after you turn the water off.
    4. Dry off with <u>your</u> towel.
    5. Put pajamas on.
    6. Put dirty clothes in hamper.
    7. Comb hair.
    8. TOTAL TIME: 15 Minutes.

These steps are age appropriate for most children 5-12 years of age. The steps you put in your list here are related to those you have from your Skill Areas.

4. Make sure that the chart is ATTRACTIVE. This means some simple artwork. <u>Don't be concerned about being an artist</u>. You can cut pictures out of magazines for some of the art work. In fact, it is best to have your child involved with decorating the chart. If you include your child in decorating the chart they will feel much more a part of the learning process

The following are some ideas for Cue Charts for Skill Areas. There are some pages of examples of some Cue Charts after the section on "Putting it All Together".

PERSONAL SKILLS:
- Room Chore Chart
- Bath Check Chart

HOUSEHOLD SKILLS:
- Living Room Chore Chart
- Kitchen Chore Chart
- Animal Care Chart
- Yard Work Chore Chart

EDUCATIONAL SKILLS:
- School Responsibilities

SOCIAL SKILLS:
- House Rules
- Public Behavior

CHAPTER SUMMARY: Learning how to Target Behaviors that you want your child change or learn is a crucial part of effective parenting. Learn to recognize the difference between Behavior Excesses (Inappropriate Behaviors) and Behavior Deficits (Desirable Skills which occur very little or not at all). As you learn to identify the difference between the two you will be able to Pin Point (Target Behaviors) more accurately those behaviors you want your child to learn or change. There are two ways to change Behaviors Excesses (Inappropriate Behaviors). One way is to ignore the inappropriate behavior and Positively Reinforce an appropriate behavior that is incompatible with the inappropriate behavior. The other way is to punish the inappropriate behavior and Positively Reinforce an appropriate behavior that is incompatible with the inappropriate behavior. The "Index of Behavior Excesses" will help you clearly identify inappropriate behaviors quickly. A Behavior Deficit is a Desired Appropriate Behavior that occurs very little or not at all. The "Desired Behavior" can be seen as a "Skill" and therefore taught as a Skill. Two of the greatest tools for teaching Skills is the Incentive Charts and Cue Charts. These two methods are very effective ways of giving you Success in Parenting.

Putting It All Together

This last chapter is an overview of all the chapters and how to "Put It All Together". After reading all the chapters and <u>doing all the exercises</u> it is now time for you to implement what you have learned in this book. As you diligently apply the principles and methods in this book you will have Successful Parenting.

Steps to Strategies

Now that you have read the entire book and done all of the exercises in the chapters it is time for you to "Put It All Together". The following Steps will help you develop successful Strategies for carrying out what you have learned:

1. Identify the Behavior Deficits of your child that you want to work on first. Remember, the Behavior Deficits are treated as *Skills which need to be learned or strengthen*. The following Steps will help you:

    A) You can use the observation records you made of your child (for the chapter exercises) to help identify the behaviors you want your child to change or learn. You can also do new observations to go from as well.

    B) Use the "Skill Areas" in chapter 7 to help identify Target Behaviors as well. The Skill Areas include "Personal Skills", "Household Skills", "Educational Skills", and Social Skills". You can use one or all of the Skill Areas to help identify specific Skills you want to Target for your child.

2. Make your child's "Reinforcer Lists". You can use the ones you made for the chapter exercises (in Chapter 5) or make new ones. The Reinforcer Lists are crucial for motivating your child. Remember to follow all the steps laid out in the chapter.

3. Make your child's Incentive Charts. Remember to follow all of the steps in the process.Make the Cue Charts and place them in strategic places around the house.

4. Make a brief "Negative Consequences Plan". You can use the "Negative Consequence Chart" (found in Chapter 6) as a guide. This should be a very simple plan put down on paper to help guide you and give you cues, in advance, about the kinds of punishment you plan to use. Make your child aware of it, but don't spend a great deal of time dwelling on it with your child. The purpose of a Negative Consequences Plan is to give you a

consistent way of punishing your child. Your plan for Negative Consequences should be only a fraction of the size of your child's Incentive Chart / Positive Reinforcer plan.

6. Keep brief records of your child's progress. Don't make it a "paper work" project. Keep everything very simple. Keep just enough notes about his progress to help you make future decisions based on something concrete.

7. **Review the Chapters in the book about every two weeks for three months to help you evaluate your effectiveness in applying the principles and methods.**

All of the principles and methods presented in this book have been used by hundreds of Behavior Specialists all over the world with hundreds of thousands of children and adults. The more you become familiar with these principles and practice these methods, the more you will experience Success in Parenting.

Incentive Charts, School Card, & Cue Charts

In this section you will find examples of Incentive *Charts, School Card, and Cue Charts.* These examples will help you design the tools you need to motivate your child and monitor his or her progress. The charts in this book are in black and white for publishing reasons. Remember to use lots of color when you and your child make his charts. Remember that children respond to the charts best when they have a part in making the charts.

Kevin Smith's School Card

For The Week Of: March 9, 2014 to March 13, 2014

Responsibility	Monday	Tuesday	Wednesday	Thursday	Friday
Present Card To Teacher					
Follow Directions					
Complete Class Work					
Complete Homework					
Work Quietly At Desk					
Keep Hands To Self					
STARS ☆ ☆					

Teacher's Signature at end of the week:
** Please initial each square for successes only.

The School Card

The School Card has been a very effective tool for many students in many schools. Used correctly it can produce wonderful results. There are some variations of the School Card used. We are going to use a School Card based on a *Positive Model* of Behavior Modification. The Positive Model uses Positive Reinforcement. In a Positive Model only correct responses (Desired Behaviors) are recognized, incorrect responses (Undesirable Behaviors) are not. This kind of School Card is a type of INCENTIVE CHART. Positive Reinforcement is accomplished by the teacher initialing each square as the student meets the criteria for each Target Behavior each day.

The School Card consist of categories of Target Behaviors listed in boxes on the left hand side of the card. As your child accomplishes the criteria for each Target Behavior then the teacher puts his <u>initials</u> in each box for that day. The teacher's initials in each box serve as Positive Reinforcers because they represent activities and things (Positive Reinforcers) your child can earn when he gets home from school.

Earning Activities and Things (Positive Reinforcers): Some Target Behaviors have a criteria of 100% and other Target Behaviors have a criteria of 80%. This means that for some Target Behaviors your child will need to complete the Target Behavior 100% before he earns the teacher's initials in the square. These are the Target Behaviors that have to do with academics. Some examples are: "presenting the school card to the teacher", "homework", and "class work". The Target Behaviors that require a criteria of 80% are the ones that have to do with social behavior. Some examples of social behaviors are: "keep hands to self", "work quietly at desk", "raise hand to talk", etc. An 80% criteria for these social behaviors means that your child need to engage in these Social Target Behaviors at least 80% of school day. This is a criteria which is the standard set by Behavioral Psychologist for Social Target Behaviors.

In order to use the School Card with your child in his school setting you will need to communicate and coordinate with his teacher what the School

Card is for and how it's used. It is vital that your child take the School Card to school each day. The School Card is your greatest tool for Daily communication between you and your child's teacher. Part of your role as the parent is making sure that your child has the card when he leaves for school in the morning. Do not leave it up to your child. It is the teacher's responsibility to ask your child for his card when he gets to school in the morning. It is also the teacher's responsibility to make sure your child has it at the end of the school day to take home.

The best way to introduce the School Card system to your child's teacher is by letter. It is also advisable that talk with your child's teacher about it in person if you can. If you can't talk with your child's teacher in person you should try to reach her by phone. In order for the School Card system to work effectively there must be good communication between you and your child's teacher.

In the letter to your child's teacher explain to her that you are interested in using a well-tested School Card system to improve your child's behavior in class. Include copies of the School Card System Information Sheets with your letter. These Information Sheets will tell your child's teacher WHAT the School card system is and HOW to use it.

SCHOOL CARD SYSTEM INFORMATION SHEET

The Purpose of the School Card: The purpose of the School Card is to *monitor* and *reinforce* APPROPRIATE behavior. It acts as a *visual cue* as well as an *Incentive Chart* for the student. The School Card focuses in on and capitalizes on Target Behaviors (Desired Behaviors). It is based on a *Positive Model* of Behavior Modification. The Positive Model uses Positive Reinforcement. In a Positive Model only correct responses (Desired Behavior) are recognized and incorrect responses (Undesirable Behaviors) are ignored.

How the School Card works: The School Card consist of Target Behaviors listed in boxes on the left hand side of the card. As the student accomplishes the criteria for each Target Behavior then his teacher puts her initials in the corresponding box each day. The teacher's *initials* serve as *Positive Reinforcers* because they represent activities and things (Positive Reinforcers) the student can earn when he gets home.

Earning Activities and Things (Positive Reinforcers):   Some Target Behaviors have a criteria of 100% and other Target Behaviors have a criteria of 80%. This means that for some Target Behaviors the student will need to complete the Target Behavior 100% before he earns the teacher's initials in the square. These are the Target Behaviors that have to do with academics. Some examples are: "presenting the school card to the teacher", "homework", and "class work". *This means that if the student has completed 100% his homework or class work then he has met the criteria for these Target Behaviors and the teacher initials the corresponding boxes.*

 The Target Behaviors that require a criteria of 80% are the ones that have to do with social behavior. Some examples of social behaviors are: "keep hands to self", "work quietly at desk", "raise hand to talk", etc.   An 80% criteria for these social behaviors means that the student needs to engage in these Social Target Behaviors at least 80% of the school day. This is a criteria which is the standard set by Behavioral Psychologist for Social Target Behaviors. *This means that if the student engages in these Social Target Behaviors 80% of the time during the school day the teacher initials the corresponding boxes.*

School Card Responsibility: It is the responsibility of the parent to make sure the student has the card when the student leaves for school in the morning. It is the teacher's responsibility to ask the student for the card each morning. At the end of each school day the teacher initials the card and hands the card back to the student and makes sure the student has the card ready to take home (secured in book bag or back pack, etc.). When the student arrives home the parent (or person caring for the child) ask for the School Card for review.

DAILY INCENTIVE CHART

Todd: Come fly with us
For in the morning!!
Opportunities!!!!

Earn Stars

Responsibility	Monday	Tuesday	Wednesday	Thursday	Friday
Out of Bed: - On first call wake up at 6:30am					
Get Dressed: - Underwear - Pants - Shirts - Socks - Shoes - Done by 6:50am					
Make Bed Comb Hair - Done by 7:05am					
Eat and Finish Breakfast by 7:20am					
Brush Teeth and ready for School by 7:35am					
If you get 3 checks you get a star!!					

Todd: These Are The Opportunities You Can Earn For Each Day With Your STARS!

1 star

- Free Play
- Watch T.V.
- Watch Video
- Play Outside
- Play Next Door
- Arts & Crafts

2 stars

- Ride Bike
- Skateboard
- Free Play
- Play Outside
- Play Next Door
- Watch T.V.
- Watch Video
- Slot Cars
- 1 Soda
- Arts & Crafts
- Nintendo (30 minutes)

3 stars

- Fly Kite
- Ride Bike
- Free Play
- Play Outside
- Play Next Door
- Watch T.V.
- Watch Video
- Arts & Crafts
- 1 Soda
- Slot Cars
- Bake Cookies
- Lego Set
- Nintendo (1 Hour)
- Stay up an Extra 30 Minutes

Todd: These Are The Opportunities You Can Earn Once A Week With Your STARS!

3

CHOOSE TWO:

- Go To The Park
- Spend $1.00 At The Dollar Store

4 ★★★★

CHOOSE TWO:

- Go To The Park
- Spend $2.00 At The Dollar Store
- Spend The Night At A Friend's House
- Have A Friend Spend The Night.
- Stay Up An Extra Hour At Night.

5

CHOOSE TWO:

- Go To The Park
- Spend The Night At A Friend's House.
- Have A Friend Spend The Night.
- Spend $2.50 At The Dollar Store

.

Lisa: Come fly with us to have fun!

Lisa: The Butterflies you earn each day can earn Heart Stickers.

Monday	Tuesday	Wednesday	Thursday	Friday

With Four Heart Stickers You Can Earn:

CHOOSE TWO FROM THIS LIST:
- Go swimming.
- Go to cousin Jamie's house.
- Rent a special video.

With Five Butterfly Stickers You Can Earn:

CHOOSE TWO FROM THIS LIST:
- Go Swimming.
- Go to Cousin Jamie's house.
- Rent a special video.
- Spend the night at a friend's house or have a friend stay overnight.
- Bake cookies.

WEEKLY INCENTIVE CHART

Karson: Put Stars all the boxes this month and you can go

Karson: Put A Star In A Box Each Time You Get A Red Check Mark On Your Weekly "Chore" Chart!

★	★	★	★			

Karson: Put A Star In A Box Each Time You Get A Red Check Mark On Your Weekly "Following Directions And Self Control" Chart!

★	★	★	★			

Karson: Put A Star In A Box Each Time You Get A Red Check Mark On Your Weekly "Following Directions and Self Control" Chart!

Put Stars In All The Boxes This Month
And You Earn $8.00 To Spend At The Dollar Store!

Lisa: Fill In The Boxes With Dove Stickers This Month And You Earn Your Trip To The Beach!

Lisa: each time you earn a Heart Sticker on your Weekly chart you earn a Dove Sticker to put in a box!

Kevin: Fill In The Stars This Month And Earn A Trip To The Zoo!

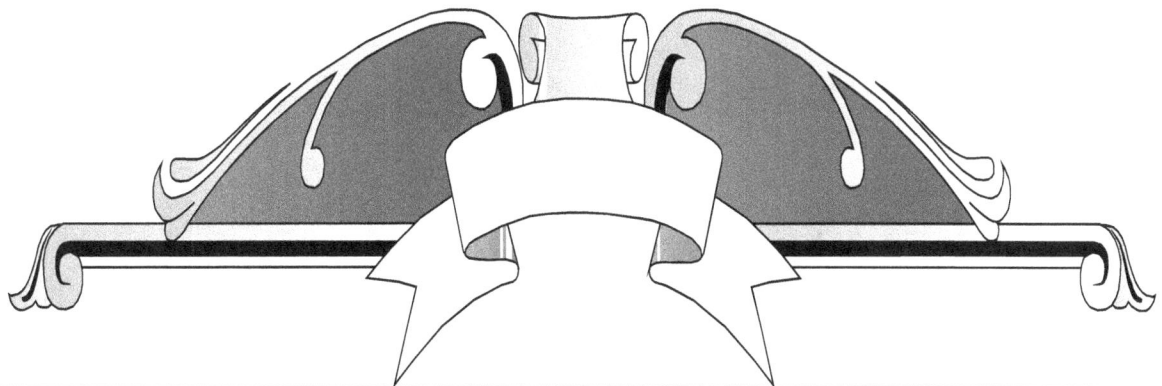

LIVING ROOM CHORE

1. Put away all items which do not belong in the living room (Items which belong to individuals, put in their room on their bed.

2. Vacuum living room area. Move furniture items to vacuum as needed.

3. Dust once a month at the direction of the adult-in-charge.

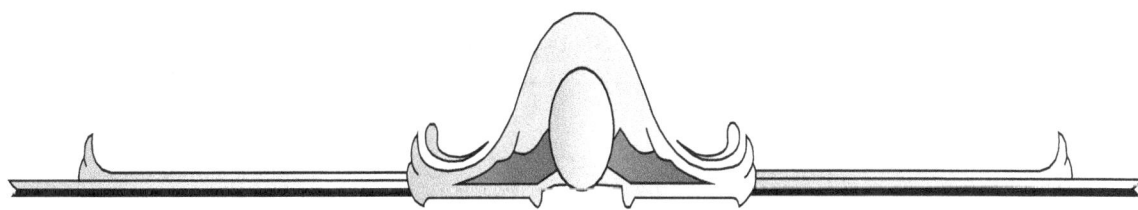

Room Check

1. Make Bed

2. Fold and put away laundry. Make sure your drawers are organized (pants with pants, shirts with shirts, etc.) Make sure school clothes are laid out for the next school day.

3. Take dirty clothes to the laundry room.

4. Put away your toys and organize your shelves.

5. Clean up the floor:
    - Pick up all items off the floor.
    - Vacuum on Fridays.

TIME: This is a 10 minute chore. It is done before breakfast and before bedtime.

*** Bath Check ***

1. Take off clothes and put them in the hamper.

2. Take a bath/shower.

3. Hang up wash-rag after you turn off water.

4. Dry off with your towel.

5. Put pajamas on.

6. Put dirty clothes in hamper.

7. Comb hair.

TOTAL TIME: 15 minutes.

Kitchen Chore

1. Rinse dishes and put them in the dishwasher.

2. Wipe down table, stove, and counters.

4. Wash pots and pans which don't fit into the dishwasher and put them away.

5. Wipe down dirty cabinet areas.

6. Sweep the floor.

7. TIME FOR CHORE: 15 Minutes. The adult-in-charge may extend the time for large meals.

House Rules

- To earn activities and opportunities you must do your chores completely and on time with a pleasant attitude.

- Knock on bedroom and bathroom doors before entering.

- Keep your personal items in your room.

- If you want to lock your bedroom door get permission from an adult-in-charge.

- Room check must be done BEFORE breakfast.

- Room check is done again 30 minutes before bedtime.

- The only name you can call people is their real name.

- When the adults-in-charge ask you to do something you need to do it immediately and with a pleasant attitude.

- Keep our hands and feet to ourselves.

- You must ask permission to enter another person's bedroom.

- The decisions of the adults-in-charge must be accepted with a pleasant attitude.

- You need to get permission to play with other people's toys or personal belongings.